Vieille Moustache

The Barb and the Bridle

A Handbook of Equitation for Ladies

Vieille Moustache

The Barb and the Bridle
A Handbook of Equitation for Ladies

ISBN/EAN: 9783337111977

Printed in Europe, USA, Canada, Australia, Japan

Cover: Foto ©ninafisch / pixelio.de

More available books at **www.hansebooks.com**

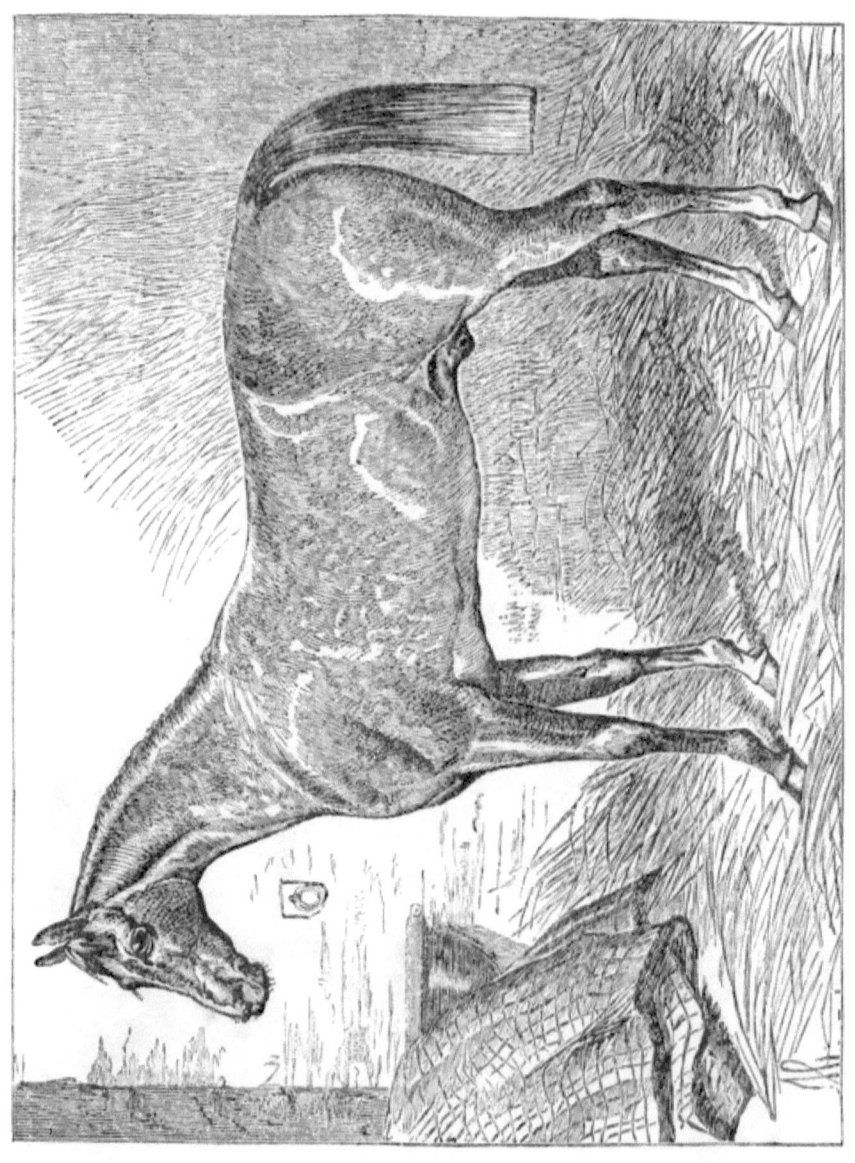

THE LADY'S HORSE.

THE

BARB AND THE BRIDLE;

A

HANDBOOK

OF

EQUITATION FOR LADIES,

AND

MANUAL OF INSTRUCTION IN THE SCIENCE OF RIDING, FROM THE PREPARATORY SUPPLING EXERCISES ON FOOT, TO THE FORM IN WHICH A LADY SHOULD RIDE TO HOUNDS.

Reprinted from " The Queen " Newspaper.

BY "VIEILLE MOUSTACHE."

LONDON:
THE "QUEEN" OFFICE, 346, STRAND.

1874.

INTRODUCTION.

HAVING received numerous applications from ladies desirous of information, as to the true principles and practice of equitation, I venture to put before the public, in book form, a series of articles which appeared originally in the columns of the *Queen* newspaper on ladies' riding.

Commencing with the calisthenic practices so necessary to a young lady before beginning her mounted lessons, these papers enter into every detail (less those of the *Haut Ecole de Manège*) connected with the science of riding as it should be acquired by all who wish to become efficient horsewomen. As the rules laid down are precisely those upon which I have successfully instructed a great number of ladies, as my experience is of many years' standing, and acquired in the best schools in Europe, I trust the following pages may prove useful;

for, while it is quite true that neither man nor woman can learn to ride by simply reading a book on the subject, still a carefully-compiled manual of equitation is always a ready means of refreshing the memory upon points of importance in the art, which, however clearly explained by the oral instruction of a first-class master, may yet in time escape the recollection of the pupil.

"VIEILLE MOUSTACHE."

THE BARB AND THE BRIDLE.

CHAPTER I.

RIDING, considered as a means of recreation, as a promoter of health, or as the best mode in which to display to the greatest advantage beauty and symmetry of face and form, is perhaps unequalled among the many accomplishments necessary to a lady.

Out of doors croquet may be interesting as a game, and fascinating enough when a lady has an agreeable partner, but as an exercise physically its healthfulness is doubtful.

There is too much standing about, often on damp grass, too little real exertion to keep the circulation up properly, and too many intervals of quiescence, wherein a lady stands perfectly still (in a very graceful attitude no doubt) long enough in the chill evening air to create catarrh or influenza.

Archery, although a far more graceful exercise than croquet, is open to the same objection as regards danger of taking cold.

Skating, though both healthful and elegant, is so seldom available as scarcely to be reckoned among the exercises beneficial to ladies. Moreover, it is attended with considerable danger in many cases.

To be well is to look well. Healthy physical exertion is indispensable to the former state, and in no way can it be so well secured as by riding. Mounted on a well-broken, well-bred horse, and cantering over a breezy down, or trotting on the soft sward, on the way to covert, a lady feels a glow of health and flow of spirits unattainable by any other kind of out or in door recreation.

That the foregoing truths are fully appreciated by the ladies of the Upper Ten Thousand is abundantly proved by the goodly gathering of fair and aristocratic equestrians to be seen in Rotten Row during the London season, and at every fashionable meet of hounds in the kingdom in the winter time.

Nor is riding confined to those only whose names figure in the pages of "Burke" or "Debrett." Within the last twenty years the wives and daughters of professional men and wealthy tradesmen, who were content formerly to take an airing in a carriage, have taken to riding on horseback. And they are quite right. It is not (with management) a bit more expensive, while it is beyond comparison the most agreeable and salubrious mode of inhaling the breeze.

The daughter of the peer, or other great grandee of the country, may be almost said to be a horsewoman to the manner born. Riding comes as naturally to her as it does to her brothers. Both clamber up on their ponies, or are lifted on, almost as soon as they can walk, and consequently "grow" into their riding, and become at fifteen or sixteen years of age as much at home in the saddle as they are on a sofa. In the hunting field they see the best types of riding extant, male and female, and learn to copy their style and mode of handling their horses, while oral instruction of the highest order is always at hand to supplement daily practice. To the great ladies of England, then, all hints on the subject would be superfluous. Most of them justly take great pride in their riding, spare no pains to excel in it, and are thoroughly successful.

In fact, it is the one accomplishment in which they as far surpass the women of all other countries in the world as they outvie them in personal beauty.

A German or French woman possibly may hold her own with an Englishwoman in a ball room or a box at the opera; but put her on horseback, and take her to the covert side, she is "not in it" with her English rivals.

Although the advantages and opportunities I speak of, however, render words of advice upon female equitation unnecessary to ladies of the *sangre azul*, I trust they may be found useful to others who may not have had such opportunities.

In the upper middle classes nothing is more probable than the marriage of one of the daughters of the house with a man whose future lot may be cast in the colonies, where if a woman cannot ride she will be sorely at a loss. Unlike the ladies of high degree above alluded to, the daughter of a man in good position in the middle class will often not have opportunities of learning to ride until she is fifteen or sixteen, and by this time the youthful frame, supple as it may appear, has acquired (so to speak) "a set," which at first renders riding far from agreeable; because it calls into action whole sets of muscles and ligaments heretofore rarely brought into play, or rather only partially so. Hence the unpleasant stiffness that always follows the first essays of the tyro in riding of the age I speak of, and which painful feeling too often so discourages beginners that they give up the thing in disgust.

Now this unpleasant consequence of the first lessons may be easily obviated by the following means. Bearing in mind that pain or stiffness is the result of want of *supplesse*, the first desideratum is to acquire this most desirable elasticity. To accomplish this, three months before the pupil is put on horseback she should begin a course of training in suppling and extension motions on foot, precisely similar to those drilled into a cavalry recruit in the army. No amount of dancing will do what is required. Even the professional *danseuse*, with her constant exercise of the *ronde de jambe*, never possesses that mobile action of the waist and play of the joints of the upper part of the figure so thoroughly to be acquired by the exercises I speak of, which also have the further greater advantage of giving development and expansion to the chest. I therefore respectfully advise every careful mother, who is desirous of seeing her daughters become accomplished horsewomen, before taking them to the riding master (of whom more hereafter), in the first place to employ a good drill master.

Possibly, the young ladies may have had drill instruction at school; but experience tells me that such instruction is too often slurred over, or only practised at such long intervals that its effect is confined to causing the pupil to walk upright and carry herself well—a very desirable matter, but not all that is requisite as a preparation for riding.

Drill, to be effective for the above purposes, *should be practised daily*. The course of instruction should begin with very short lessons, lasting not more than twenty minutes at first; but these, *given in the presence of mamma*, should be *most rigidly and minutely carried out, otherwise they are useless*. They should gradually be increased in length, according to the strength of the pupil, until she can stand an hour's drilling without fatigue. The course should include instruction in the use of dumb-bells, very carefully given. The weight of these should in no case exceed seven pounds for a young lady of fifteen or sixteen, and may judiciously be confined to three and four pounds for those of a more tender age. The great use of dumb-bells is to give flexibility to the shoulder joints and expansion to the chest. The first lessons should not last more than five minutes, and in no case be continued an instant after the pupil exhibits the slightest symptom (easily discernable) of fatigue.

Of the course of drill instruction, the lessons called the "extension motions" are the most effectual in promoting flexibility of the whole figure; but they must be gone into by very gradual and careful induction, and their effect will then be not only beneficial, but pleasant to the pupil.

As it is possible that this may meet the eye of some lady who resides where no eligible drill master is available, I propose in my next chapter to give a programme of the exercises I speak of, which may then be practised under the superintendence of the lady herself or her governess. But in all cases where the services of a competent and thoroughly practised drill master are to be had it is always best to employ them.

Simple as the instruction may appear, the art of imparting it has to be acquired in a school where the most minute attention is paid to every detail, where nothing is allowed to be done in a careless or slovenly manner, and where (so to speak) the pupil is never asked to read before he can spell. It is this jumping *in medias* with beginners in riding that so often causes mischief and disgusts the pupil, who begins by thinking that it is the easiest thing in the world to ride well, but when she is put on horseback finds to her dismay that it is anything but easy until acquired by practice and thoroughly good instructions.

CHAPTER II.

I PROCEED now to describe the suppling and extension exercises I have before alluded to.

These are simple enough in themselves, certain not to be forgotten when once learnt, and easy to impart in the way of instruction. Their great efficacy depends, however, upon the judgment with which the instructor varies them, so as to call into action alternately opposite sets of muscles and ligaments, as it is by such a process only

Fig. 1.   Fig. 2.

that complete *supplesse* can be attained. The first suppling practice is performed as follows: Place the pupil in a position perfectly upright, the heels close together, the toes at an angle of 45 (military regulation), the figure well drawn up from the waist, the shoulders thrown back, chest advanced, the neck and head erect, arms hanging perpendicularly from the shoulder, elbows slightly bent, the weight of the body thrown upon the front part of the foot.

Then the instruction should be given thus: On the word "one," bring both hands smartly up to the full extent of the arms, in front and above the forehead, the tips of the fingers joining (Fig. 1); on the word "two," throw the hands sharply backwards and downwards until they meet behind the back (Fig. 2). This exercise should be

Fig. 3.   Fig. 4.

commenced slowly, and gradually increased in rapidity until the pupil can execute it with great quickness for several minutes consecutively. The object is to throw the shoulders well back and give expansion to the chest.

Second practice.—On the word "one," bring the hands together (from their position perpendicular from the shoulder) in front of the figure, the tips of the fingers joining (Fig. 3). On the word "two," raise the hands, still joined, slowly above and slightly in front of the head, to the full extent of the arms (Fig. 4). "Three," separate the hands, and, turning the palms upwards, lower them to the level of the shoulders, the arms fully extended (Fig. 5). Simultaneously with the lowering of the hands the heels should be raised slowly from the ground, so as to bring the weight of the body upon the toes. On the word "four," lower the hands gradually to the sides, carrying them at the same time well to the rear (Fig. 6). The heels are

Fig. 5.   Fig. 6.

also to be lowered to the ground as the hands are carried backwards. This exercise should always be done slowly, as its object is the gradual flexing and suppling of the shoulder and elbow joints, and giving mobile action to those of the feet. In using dumb-bells the first practice with them may be identical with the above, the dumb-bells being grasped firmly in the centre.

Third practice.—On the word "one," close the hands firmly by the sides; "two," raise them up quietly, bending the elbows until the hands are touching the points of the shoulders (Fig. 7); "three," carry the hands, still firmly closed, forwards and upwards, to the full extent of the arms, well above and a little in front of the head (Fig. 8); "four," bring the hands with a quick, sharp motion down to the level of the shoulders, carrying the elbows well to the rear (Fig. 9). The first two motions of this exercise should be performed very slowly, the last very rapidly. It can also be practised with advantage with the dumb-bells, and is then of great service in strengthening and developing the muscles of the chest and arms.

Fig. 7.   Fig. 8.

There are a great many other suppling practices, but the above, varied occasionally by the use of the dumb bells, will be found sufficient for all practical purposes.

Coming now to the extension exercises, I select the third as being most effective. 1st motion. Bring the hands together in front of the figure, as in the second suppling practice, the points of the fingers joining, the whole frame erect and well drawn up from the waist.
2. Raise the hands slowly above the head to the full extent of the

arms, turn the palms of the hands outwards, and lock the thumbs together, the right thumb within the left (Fig. 10). 3. Keeping the body, head, and neck perfectly erect, place the head between the arms, the thumbs still firmly locked together. 4. *Keeping the knees perfectly straight*, lower the hands, and bend the back gradually and very slowly forward and downwards, until the points of the fingers touch the instep (Fig. 11). 5. Raise the body and head (the latter still between the arms), quietly up in the same slow time, bringing

Fig. 9.   Fig. 10.

the hands again well above the head (Fig. 12). 6. Lower the hands gradually (turning the palms upwards), first to the level of the shoulders, making a momentary pause there, and then quietly to the sides, carrying the hands in their descent from the shoulder as much as possible to the rear, while the weight of the body is thrown entirely upon the front of the foot.

In this exercise all depends upon keeping the knee joints perfectly straight, and the head, in the bending-down movement, as much as possible between the arms.

The object of the practice is to give suppleness to the waist, freedom to the knee joint by well suppling the ligaments at the back of the knee, and at the same time to expand the chest. For these purposes, if carefully and judiciously carried out, it is most effective, calling alternately upon every portion of the frame wherein suppleness is indispensable to easy and graceful riding.

Great care should be taken not to hurry this lesson, and if the pupil is of a figure that renders it difficult for her to reach her instep

Fig. 11.   Fig 12.

in bending down, it should not be insisted on; but it is necessary that she should bend the back as much as possible *without bending the knees*, as any yielding of the knee joint destroys the whole value of the exercise.

To perform the above named practices comfortably, the pupil should wear a loose dress which throws no constraint upon any part of the figure. Slippers, too, are better than boots, as the latter confine the foot and ankle too much for complete liberty of movement.

The duration of any of these lessons should at first be carefully proportioned to the strength of the learner, and gradually increased as to time day by day, until she can stand an hour's work without fatigue; but be the lesson long or short, it should be practised every day.

It will be found that, with plenty of fresh air and walking exercise, the pupil, by the aid of these suppling and extension practices, will develope rapidly in elasticity of movement and in general health, and that a couple or three months of such preparation will help her very much as an introduction to her course of equitation.

Any good drill master who might be employed to "set up" a young lady would most likely teach her all the above, and much more; but I have ventured to detail these practices, assuming that a family may be located in a neighbourhood in which no such man is available, in which case the exercise can be imparted and superintended by the governess of the family. These ladies are always clever and intelligent enough to master in a few minutes such very simple details as those above described.

Before quitting this subject a word about gymnastics may not be out of place. Many heads of families consider them highly beneficial when practised with bars and similar apparatus. My experience induces me to differ from this notion, and I believe my view of the matter would be borne out by the highest medical authority.

For boys even, gymnastic exercises should be most carefully watched, in order that no undue strain should be thrown upon the yet unset muscle and cartilage of the frame. For young ladies I believe gymnastics to be not only unnecessary, but injurious, and that every practical result desirable can be arrived at by the use of such exercises as I have endeavoured to describe, varied occasionally by the moderate use of the dumb-bells, a few minutes of which at one time is always sufficient. Where there is a number of young people together, there is sure to be a tendency to outdo each other whenever physical exercises of any kind are introduced; and, while it is easy enough to control the pupils in the simple suppling practices I speak of, it is very difficult for any but the most experienced persons to determine how far a young lady may go without injury to herself in the exercises of the horizontal bars or trapeze ropes. If any kind of gymnastic exercises are allowed for a young lady, the best, in my opinion, are those practised with the "Ranelagh," because no hurtful strain can possibly be thrown upon the pupil; and for boys I believe the Ranelagh to be a first-rate invention, as is also the "Parlour Gymnasium," and several others on similar principles, which ignore the practice of the bars.

The full practice of the gymnasium, however, for young men whose frames have attained a certain amount of maturity, is no doubt good if not carried to excess. I speak, however, only of young ladies of tender age.

Assuming then, that our pupil has been prepared for riding as above described, let us proceed to consider the style of dress most suitable for her early attempts in the saddle. For very young ladies, say under twelve years of age, I believe in hair cut short in preference to flowing locks, because the latter are very apt to blow into the eyes and seriously interfere with riding. For the very juvenile equestrian tyro, the hat should be one that fastens under the chin with ribbon or something *that is not elastic*. Nothing is more important in beginning with young people on horseback than to give them confidence, and nothing so completely puts them out as anything loose about the head. For young ladies over fifteen or sixteen, hats which are fastened to the hair may be worn. But, having regard to the progress of the pupil rather than to appearance, I recommend every beginner, no matter what her age, to leave no doubt about the security of her headdress. As regards riding habits, to begin with, while they should fit sufficiently to indicate the outline of the lady's figure, all tightness should be avoided. Tight habits are very sightly to the eye; but, in common with tight corsets, steel or whalebone anywhere about the dress is fatal to that perfect liberty of movement so essential to success in a beginner.

Loose jackets of course should not be worn, because the instructor would be unable to see in what form his pupil was sitting. Nothing is better, in the first place, than a jacket, of any coarse material the rider chooses, made in the ordinary form, with plenty of room, especially about the waist and shoulders. The skirt should not be too redundant or too long, as in the latter case it is apt to get trodden on by the horse, and in windy weather blows about, to the great annoyance of the rider. A skirt that reaches about 12in. below the foot is amply long. As to breadth, it should be just large enough to give space to move easily in. A more voluminous garment is unsightly. The skirt, made independent of the jacket, should fasten under it with a broad band. No clothing should be worn under the skirt except riding trousers. Under-skirts of any kind will utterly spoil the appearance of the fair equestrian, and render her ride one of discomfort.

Riding trousers, the making of which should only be entrusted to people who are well accustomed to it, may be made of cloth or chamois leather, booted with cloth.

The boots, whether Wellingtons (if they are not out of date), side springs, or lace boots, should be made purposely for riding. Fashion is imperious, and that of the present day dictates a boot with a very high, narrow heel, and a waist which is almost triangular; both are quite unsuited for riding. The heel of a riding boot should be quite as broad as the foot of the wearer, and should come well forward into the waist, after the manner of a man's hunting boot, and the waist itself should be perfectly flat, so as to give a firm level bearing on the stirrup-iron. A sharp, narrow-waisted boot will be found not only impossible to keep in place in the iron, but will hurt the sole of the foot very much.

Of spurs (very necessary in an advanced state of proficiency, and inadmissible, of course, to a beginner) I shall say something hereafter.

Of gloves, the best kind for riding is a dogskin glove or gauntlet *two sizes too large*. Six and a-half kid gloves do not admit of sufficient freedom in the hand properly to manipulate the reins.

The pupil should be provided with a straight riding whip which is not too flexible, because with a very supple whip she may inadvertently touch the horse at the wrong time and upset him.

Having said thus much as to the equipment of our fair tyro, I leave all observations as to dress fit for the hunting-field, or such promenade riding as that of Rotten Row, for a future paper, and proceed to say something about that very important consideration, the matter of the riding master.

In the first place, then, it is necessary that the professor of equitation should be one who has been regularly brought up to his business. If such a man is not within reach, then I submit that it is better to entrust the riding education of the young lady to any staid middle-aged gentleman who is a thoroughly good horseman, and who will undertake the task *con amore*. If the gentleman has daughters of his own, all the better. I do not recommend young men for the office, because, naturally enough, they are more likely to be engrossed with the charms of their pupils than the progress they are making with their riding. Youthful preceptors, too, have a tendency to "make the pace a trifle too good," and there are not even wanting instances where they have "bolted" with their pupils altogether. This by the way.

To return to the professional riding master. I may add that, in addition to thoroughly understanding his craft, he should be a man of education and a gentleman. Of such men there are several in the metropolis; in the provinces they are few and far between. In most of our fashionable watering-places one sees very neatly got-up horsey-looking men, duly booted, spurred, and moustached, tittuping along with a small troop of young ladies, who, with their skirts ballooned out with the fresh breeze from the "briny," and "sitting all over the saddle," are making themselves very uncomfortable, when they could have enjoyed the bracing air just as well, for less money, in an open fly. The riding master, in all probability, has promoted himself from the office of pad groom. He knows how to saddle and turn out a lady's horse, and how to put the lady into the saddle; he knows, also, the cheapest market in which to go for fashionable-looking screws upon which to mount his customers. There his qualifications as a riding master end. The inductive steps by which a lady should be taught, the reason for everything she is asked to do, the "aids" by which she should control her horse and establish a good understanding with him, are all sealed mysteries to the stamp of man I speak of. From such men and their ten-pound screws there is nothing to be learnt in the way of riding.

Assuming, then, that some of my fair readers may be so placed as to render access to a professional riding master impossible, I have ventured upon this brief manual of "Equitation for Ladies," because I believe that there are many gentlemen, good horsemen, who would willingly undertake the teaching of their young friends, but that the former are unacquainted with the readiest way of going to work. Let me hope that the following may be of use in such case, both to preceptor and pupil. Addressing myself first to the former, let me advise him to be guided from first to last by the following maxims: 1st. Never do anything to shake the confidence or nerve of your pupil, and never give away a chance of doing it to the horse she rides. 2nd. Never talk to her about lesson No. 2 until she thoroughly understands lesson No. 1. While tittuping hacks are useless, and it is necessary to have an animal, even for a beginner, that has still plenty of life, vigour, and action in him, such a horse requires to be thoroughly well-broken to carry a woman, and should have plenty of work, so as to do away with the possibility of his flirting when she is mounted. It should be borne in mind that, although a woman who has had years of practice will be equally at home on almost every horse upon which you can put her, yet only a particular stamp of animal is adapted to carry her in her earlier essays.

Let me endeavour to give my idea of him. In height he should be from 15.2 to 15.3. A very tall woman may look better on a taller horse, but it is rarely that one finds an animal over 15.3 with the requisite proportions to ensure good action. Colour is of little account, except that grey horses in the summer time part with their coats so freely as to spoil a lady's habit. Quality is indispensable. A three-part-bred horse, however, is the best, because he is likely to have more substance in the right place than a thoroughbred. A good blood-like head and neck are warranty for fashion. Good shoulders, in the ordinary acceptation of the term, are not always good shoulders for a lady's horse, because while they should be clean and sloping as to the scapula, the withers should not be too fine. A little thickness there causes a side saddle to fit better for the comfort of the rider. There should be plenty of depth in the girth and rare good back ribs, for a woman's riding calls very much on a horse's power. A short back is not conducive to ease for the rider, whatever it may be as to the staying powers of the horse. On the contrary, what is generally called a long-backed horse carries a lady most pleasantly; but there must be plenty of power in the quarters, muscular upper thighs, and strong hocks. The quarters, too, should be good, and the setting on of the tail such as finishes the topping of the horse well, and gives him a fashionable appearance. If conjoined to the above-named points he stands on moderately short legs, with plenty of bone, and has good round and sound feet, he will be found as nearly as possible what is required.

CHAPTER III.

If a horse has been broken, so as to be obedient to the hand and leg of a man, and steady to sights and sounds, it is considered by many that the animal has only to be ridden with a skirt, and accustomed to strike off without hesitation with its off legs in the canter, and it is fit to carry a lady.

This is a great mistake. It is true that teaching it to canter collectedly with its off legs is necessary, as well as habituating it to the skirt, but there are other and important matters to be considered which are too often overlooked.

In the first place, a man, to break a horse properly for a lady, must be sufficiently well up at his craft to train the animal to obey the lightest possible application of the aids of the leg; because a lady, having but one leg to the horse, cannot give him the same amount of support that can be given by a man, who applies both.

To supply the absence of the leg on the off side, in the case of the lady, the only substitute is the whip. But all men accustomed to breaking know that the effect of the whip is altogether different from that of the leg, and that while the whip is occasionally necessary to rouse a slightly lazy horse, and put him into his bridle, in the case of one very free, or at all hot, the whip must be used with great caution by a lady. As I have remarked elsewhere, most young horses are inclined to strike off in the canter with the near leg, which is most unpleasant to the fair equestrian. To correct this, the breaker applies certain well-known aids, which it is unnecessary here to repeat. But in order to confirm the horse in his lesson of cantering with his off leg, the man must give the animal a considerable amount of support with both his own and both hands. If this is continued after the horse is advanced to the stage of breaking where the trainer begins to fit him for a lady, and carried on until she rides him, he will be far from a pleasant mount to her, because, missing the support of the man's legs, the horse will not understand the light and delicate ones which the lady will use. It is necessary, therefore, that the breaker should accustom his charge readily to obey the slightest indication of the rider's will, and then ride him in a side-saddle, in precisely the same way as he will afterwards be ridden by the lady.

I remember once seeing a man, really a capital rider in his own way, giving a lady a lesson on a horse of her own which he had broken for her. Both master and pupil were sorely puzzled—the former because the horse would not obey the hand and leg of the rider, as directed by the master, and the pupil, by finding that all she was doing produced an effect diametrically opposite to that which was intended. Perhaps the horse, too, was as much puzzled to know what to be at as either rider or master.

The animal was a very shapely chesnut, nearly thoroughbred, very good-tempered, but full of courage. Evidently he was unaccustomed to carry a lady, and was beginning to give indications that his temper was getting up. The object was to canter him to the right round the school, "going large," as it is technically called. He had trotted to the other hand well enough, and the young lady had ridden him fairly; but when turned to the reverse hand, and the word "canter" was given, he evidently missed the support afforded by the legs of a male rider. When pressed gently forward to a shortened rein, he stepped very high in his trot. "Touch him on the right shoulder with the whip sharply, miss," said the riding master. In answer to the sharp cut of the whip, the horse jumped off passionately in a canter, with his near legs first—a dangerous thing when going round the school to the right. "Stop him, miss," said the preceptor; "take him into the corner, bend his head to the right. Now the leg and whip again." The same result followed—the lady flurried as well as her horse. The riding master at last took the lady off, and mounted the horse himself; but he rode with a man's seat, not a woman's. The horse cantered collectedly and well into his bridle when the master asked him. "You see, miss, it is easy enough," said the master; "a little patience, and you will do it presently." But the second essay of the lady was as unsuccessful as the first; nay more so, as the horse was getting very angry. "What can be the reason?" at last said the lady, halting her horse; "I must be very stupid." "It is some peculiarity in your hand," said the master, soothingly; "it will be all right by-and-by." Do you think," said the lady, deferentially, "that the difference of seat —your leg on the right side—has anything to do with it?" "Not a bit," replied the preceptor. But it had all to do with it, and eventually the lady had to be put upon an old school hack for her ride in the park, leaving her own horse at the riding school.

When the lady was gone the master observed. "Most extraordinary thing! I can't get this horse to do wrong, and Miss A. cannot get him to go a yard." "Did you ever ride him in a side-saddle?" I inquired. "I? Certainly not," was the answer; "no man can break a horse in a side-saddle" (this was true enough as regards the early stages), "and," continued the professor, "I can't ride a bit in a side-saddle." The latter observation settled the matter in my mind; for it has been always clear to me that, if a man cannot acquire a true and firm seat himself on a side-saddle, it is impossible he can teach a woman to ride. He may teach her to sit square and upright on an old horse that has been carrying women for years, but "going about" on such an animal is not riding—my idea of which, as regards a lady, is, that on a horse still full of courage and action (though not too fresh or short of work) the rider should be able, by the application of aids sound in theory and practice, to render the horse thoroughly obedient to her will. This is riding. Cantering along upon an old tittuping hack is merely taking horse exercise in a mild form.

As regards a man riding in a side-saddle, I may say that some years ago a young friend of mine, now deceased—than whom there never was a better man with hounds—hunted in a side-saddle for three or four seasons before his death. He had injured his right foot so badly in a fall as to necessitate amputation at the instep, and he preferred the side-saddle seat to the awkward and disagreeable feeling occasioned by trusting to a cork foot in the off-side stirrup. Some of your readers may probably remember the dashing youngster I allude to, who was always to be seen going true and straight in the front rank, when he hunted eighteen years ago with the Royal Buckhounds. I can safely say that the horses he rode in his side-saddle were the perfection of ladies' hunters, and that he was one of the best instructors of female equitation I ever met.

I repeat, then, that before a horse can be pronounced fit to carry a lady he should have been ridden in a side-saddle for some time by a man.

Riding in this way, the breaker's first object should be to make the horse walk truly and fairly up to his bridle, without hurrying or shuffling in his pace, than which nothing is more unpleasant to a lady, especially if she is engaged in conversation with a companion. Of course it is indispensable that a horse should be a good natural walker, but at the same time the animal should be carefully taught to work right up to his bit in this most important pace; action in the others can then be easily developed.

In the trot the breaker should gradually accustom the animal to go with the least possible amount of support from the leg. This he will easily do by using a very long whip, and, when he feels the horse hanging back from his work, touching him lightly on the hind quarters instead of closing the leg.

In the foregoing I am assuming that the horse has been previously well broken, mouthed, and balanced to carry a man. To teach a horse readily to obey such delicate aids of hand or leg, as a lady can apply, I have found the following method most effectual: Use a side-saddle which has no head crutch on the off side; this gives more freedom of action to the right hand. Ride without a stirrup; your balance is sure then to be true. Use a long whip, and wear a spur on the left heel, furnished with short and not very sharp rowels. Make your horse walk well, and trot well up to his bridle, with as little leg as possible, touching him sharply with the spur if he tries to shirk his work. The long whip on the off side will prevent him from throwing his haunches in. Before cantering, collect him well. Keep his forehand well up, and his haunches under him. Keep his head well bent to the right; take him into the corner of the school or *manége*; then, keeping him up to his work rather by the aid of the spur and whip than by the leg, strike him lightly off to the right. A sharp touch of the spur behind the girth, and a light firm feeling of both reins, the inward the strongest, will cause him to strike off true. Where no riding house or walled *manége* is available, the above may be successfully carried out in a small paddock, having tolerably high fences and corners nearly square.

Manner in riding the horse at this stage of his breaking is of vital importance. The hands, while kept well back, should be light and lively; the whip and spur (never to be unnecessarily applied) should be used so as to let the horse know that they are always ready if he hangs back from his work; and the rider, sitting easily and flexibly in the saddle, should ride with spirit and vivacity, making much of the horse frome time to time as he answers with alacrity to the light and lively aids applied. A dull rider makes a dull horse, and *vice versâ*. Gradually, a well bred, good tempered animal will learn to answer smartly to the slightest indication of the rider's will, and while giving a good *appui* to the hand, will convey a most enjoyable feeling from his well-balanced elastic movement, without the necessity of strong or rough aids. In a very brief time the long whip can be dispensed with, and all inclination to throw the haunches in will cease. The animal has then acquired the *aplomb* necessary to fit him for the lady equestrian. He should then be taught by gradually inductive lessons to walk quietly up to his fences and jump freely, his haunches well under him; and subsequently to execute his leap from a steady, collected canter, without rush or hurry.

During the latter part of each lesson he should be ridden with a skirt or rug on.

He should then be accustomed to all kinds of sights and sounds, from the rattle of a wheelbarrow to the pattering file firing at a review, and the loud report of a great gun; and especially he should be habituated *to having all sorts of colours* about him.

I well remember seeing a fine horse, that had been some time in the breaker's hand, and was perfect in his mouth and paces, put a general officer and his lady into a complete fix. The lady went to a review, having been assisted into her saddle by her husband in his mufti costume before he dressed for parade. After the review; the lady dismounted to partake of luncheon in a marquee, and, after the repast, the general proceeded to put his wife on her horse; but the gallant steed by no means understood the dancing plume of red and white feathers in the officer's cocked hat, and he would none of him. He snorted, pawed the ground in terror, ran back, and did everything but stand still, although he had stood the marching past and firing well enough. Unluckily the groom had been sent home, and there was nobody in mufti on the ground who could put the lady on her saddle. Even when the general took off his cocked hat, the horse, having taken a dislike to him, would not let his master come near him. Finally, as there was no carriages on the ground, the lady had to walk a considerable distance, her horse led by an orderly. The above goes to show that to make a horse perfect for a lady, nothing likely to occur in the way of sights or sounds should be overlooked. If the horse possesses the requisite power and form to fit him for a hunter, and the lady for whom he is intended graces the hunting field with her presence, the animal should be ridden quietly in cubhunting time as often as possible, in long trots, *beside* the hounds going to covert, and accustomed gradually to the music of the "sylvan choir," to stand quietly at the covert side, and take no heed of scarlet coats. If the horse has been otherwise well broken, the above is simply a question of time and patience.

Let me now say something with regard to saddlery and appointments. The most important of these, of course, is the side-saddle, as to the form of which considerable diversity of opinion exists.

My own experiences induce me to believe in a saddle which is as nearly as possible *flat* from between the pommels to the cantle; any dip in the stretcher of the tree, while it renders the lady's seat less secure, has also the effect of throwing her weight too much upon the horse's forehand, and thus cramping his action. When a lady has acquired skill and confidence in her riding, a saddle with a very low-cut pommel on the off side is best, because it not only admits of the rider getting her hands lower (for which occasion may frequently occur), but on the off side it gives the lady and the horse a far better appearance, the high off side pommel spoiling the graceful contour of figure in both. Worked or plain off-side flaps are matters of taste, and have nothing to do with utility. The stirrup should be a Victoria, well padded. The leather should be fitted on the near side, in a similar manner to a man's stirrup leather, and be quite independent of the quarter strap. The reason for this is obvious. If you fit a lady's stirrup leather ever so carefully after she is up, you cannot tell how much the horse "will give up" in his girth after an hour's riding, or even less; and the leather which takes up on the off side may give to the extent of three or four holes, thereby greatly incommoding the rider, especially if she is in the hunting field and has to jump her horse, as it is ten to one, although she has the power of pulling up the leather herself, if, in the excitement of the chase, either she or anybody else will notice the rendering of the leather, and a drop leap may bring the rider to grief, whereas the near side arrangement is a fixture, and always reliable. For really comfortable riding, I believe also that it is quite as necessary that a saddle should be made in such proportion as to *fit the lady*, as that it should fit the horse. Even a thoroughly accomplished horsewoman cannot ride easily in a saddle that is too short from pommel to cantle, or too narrow in the seat. In either case, both discomfort and ungainly appearance are the result; while to a lady of slight *petite* figure, a saddle too long from front to rear is equally unsightly, though possibly not quite so uncomfortable to the rider. Broad girths of the best materials are indispensable. There should be three of them. The quarter strap or girth should lead from the near side fork of the tree to a buckle piece attached to a ring on the off-side quarter, the ring giving the quarter strap a better bearing. A crupper should never be used; a horse that requires one is not fit for a lady. Saddle cloths are unnecessary to a carefully-pannelled saddle, and hide the symmetry of the horse. Breastplates or neck straps may be used for hunting, or the fitting of martingales (neccesary sometimes). But the less leather about the horse, where it can be dispensed with, the better he will look.

As to bridles, as a rule, I maintain that a lady's horse properly broken should ride right into an ordinary double bridle, bit, and bridoon, the port of the bit proportioned to the contour and setting on of the horse's head and neck, as should also be the length of the cheek piece and jaw of the bit; while the question of a plain or twisted bridoon or snaffle must be regulated by the hand of the rider and the mouth of the horse. For park or promenade riding, fashion of late years inclines to a single rein bridle or "Hanoverian," or hard and sharp. No doubt they are very sightly and neat in appearance; but with a high-couraged horse they require very nice and finished hands, and in the majority of cases, in my humble opinion, are safe only for the most accomplished female riders.

I leave the question of bridle-fronts, bound with ribbon of pink, blue, or yellow, to the taste of my readers; when neatly put on and fresh, they look gay in the park. But either there or in the hunting field, I believe more in the plain leather front, as having, if I may so express it, a more workmanlike appearance.

Having now endeavoured to describe the best preparations on foot for the pupil, the style of dress most suitable for her first lessons in equitation, the stamp of horse a lady should ride, the training he should undergo for the special service required of him, and the kind of saddlery and equipment he will travel best in, in my next chapter I will attempt briefly, but minutely, to detail the first step in the riding lesson proper, namely, the form in which the pupil should approach her horse in order to be assisted into the saddle, and the mounting motions, all of which are of great importance, as each motion should be executed gracefully, without hurry, and in a well defined and finished manner. Nothing connected with riding stamps the style and *tournure* of a lady more than the fashion in which she mounts her horse and arranges her habit; it ought, in fact, to be a matter as carefully looked to by the instructor as her mode of entering a room would be to a master of deportment.

CHAPTER IV.

THE manner in which a lady should approach her horse in order to be assisted to mount should be carefully looked to by the instructor. Anything like hurry, while it is calculated to render the horse unsteady, is at the same time ungraceful, and the beginning of a bad habit always to be avoided.

Everything in the way of mounting or dismounting a horse, either by a lady or gentleman, should be done with well-defined and deliberate, although smart motions. This precision once acquired is the good habit which becomes second nature to the rider, and is so highly indicative of good manners in equitation.

To some persons the formula I am about to describe may appear too punctilious, and possibly carried to too nice a point of precision. But my idea is that in all these matters it is well to begin by *overdoing them* a little. We are all more or less prone to become careless in our carriage and bearing, both on foot and horseback, as we grow older; therefore overdoing them a trifle with young people may safely be pronounced an error on the right side.

I have frequently heard the remark that it is of no consequence how a man or woman gets upon a horse, provided they can ride when once up. I maintain that graceful riding is true riding, and that if it is worth while to ride gracefully, it is equally worth while to mount gracefully.

Let us then suppose the lady to be dressed and ready for her ride in school or *manége*. She should take the skirt of her habit in the full of both hands, holding her whip in the right; the skirt should be raised sufficiently to admit of the wearer walking freely. Then she should walk from a point in the school at right angles with her horse quietly to his shoulder, and face square to her left, standing just behind the animal's near elbow and parallel to his side. Thus facing to the front, and still holding her skirt with both hands, she should pass her whip from her right hand into the left, and "make much of her horse" by patting him on the near shoulder—the best method anybody (man or woman) can adopt as a first step to acquaintance with a strange horse; at the same time she should speak soothingly to her new equine friend. The horse should be held by a groom standing in front of him, and holding him by both reins. On the assistant approaching to lift the pupil to the saddle, the lady should return the whip to the right hand and drop her habit. She should then take the snaffle or bridoon rein in the centre with the left hand, at the end close to the buckle piece with the right, and draw them through the left until she has a light and equal feeling upon both sides of the horse's mouth. The right hand should then be placed firmly on the near side upper crutch of the saddle, the snaffle rein held between the pommel and the hand, the whip in the full of it. The left hand should then grip the reins, and the lady should resume her position square to the front, without moving her right hand or relaxing her grasp of the pommel of the saddle. The assistant (who should be *a gentleman*, not a groom) should then stoop low enough to place both his hands locked together in such a position that the pupil can place her left foot firmly on them, the left knee slightly bent. At the same time she should also place the flat of her left hand firmly on the right shoulder of the assistant, keeping her arm perfectly straight. The instructor should then give her the following directions: "On the word 'one,' bend the right knee; on the word 'two,' spring smartly up from the right foot and straighten the left knee." If the pupil executes these movements simultaneously, keeping her left elbow perfectly firm and the arm straight, the assistant can lift her with the greatest ease to the level of the saddle, where, firmly grasping the pommel, she has only to make a half turn to her left, and she is seated sideways on her horse. The assistant should then straighten the skirt down, and taking the slack of it in his left hand, lift it over the near side upper crutch while the lady turns in her saddle, and facing square to her point, lifts her right knee over the pommel, bringing her right leg close to the forepoint of the saddle, with the leg well drawn back, and the toe raised from the instep. The assistant should then place the lady's foot well home in the stirrup. Before raising the right knee over the pommel, the lady should lift the snaffle reins with her right hand high enough to admit of her moving the leg without interfering with them. The right knee being firmly placed between the pommels, and the left foot in the stirrup, the pupil should then place her right hand with the snaffle reins between the finger and thumb and the whip in the full of the hand, firmly on the off-side pommel of the saddle. She should then draw her left foot well back, and getting a firm bearing on the stirrup, raise herself well up from the saddle, leaning forward sufficiently to preserve her balance. She should then pass her left hand back, and pull her skirt well out, so that there remains no ruck or wrinkle in it, and then quietly lower herself down to the saddle again. This act of clearing the slack of the skirt is one which it is so frequently necessary for the lady to execute when riding that she should practise it frequently in her early lessons. It is true that when the assistant first places her on the horse he can arrange her habit as she rises from the saddle; but, for some time, until she has acquired firmness and perfect balance, her habit will inevitably ride up, particularly in trotting, and it is necessary that she should learn to be independent in this respect of the gentleman who attends her. Moreover, as to arrange the habit gracefully requires considerable practice, it should form a distinct part of the lesson at first when the horse is standing perfectly still, afterwards at a walk, and finally at a trot. In cantering it cannot be done.

Having arranged the hind part of her skirt, the lady should then take the front in her left hand, and pull it well forward, raising her right knee at the same time, to insure that she has perfect freedom of action for it. The left knee should then be placed firmly against the leaping crutch (or, as it is generally called, the third crutch) of the saddle; although with saddles devoid of an off-side pommel, it is, in fact, the second crutch. This important adjunct to a lady's firmness and security in riding should always be most carefully looked to by Paterfamilias when purchasing the saddle, and by the master after it is bought. I can well remember when the third crutch was unknown; and in these days, when its efficiency has been so abundantly proved, it really seems marvellous how ladies years ago could not only ride well without it, but even acquit themselves creditably in the hunting field. The secret of the matter, however, lies in this: First, although there was no third support for the rider, the off-side and near-side pommels were much closer together than those now made; the off-side one was well padded, and in most cases where ladies rode hunting it was usual to have an extra pad, which fitted on to the off-side crutch, and again narrowed the interval, according to the size of the lady, until her leg fitted tightly between the two crutches, thus giving her a very firm hold with the right knee. Nevertheless, it is evident that only the truest balance would enable the fair equestrians of those days to maintain their seats.

When a young lady is first put on horseback, I believe in anything that can give her confidence, and for this purpose the third crutch is admirable, because she finds a firm purchase between the crutch and the stirrup. As this hold, however, is apt to degenerate into a complete reliance on the third pommel, it is necessary in a more advanced stage of the lessons in equitation to use a saddle without any such support for the pupil. The third crutch, when forming part of a side-saddle, *should never be removed*, as is too frequently done by grooms for the purpose of cleaning the saddle. The crutch itself is so constructed as to screw into a socket in the tree. By constantly screwing and unscrewing it, the thread of the screw wears out; in fact, this will occur much sooner than would be supposed. The consequence is that, let the lady or her assistant turn the third crutch to what angle they may in order to suit the length and formation of the lady's leg, the crutch will not remain in its proper position, but is continually shifting, turning, and wobbling, to the great discomfort of the rider; nay, I have seen more than one case where the crutch has turned edgeways to the rider's leg, and caused severe pain and bruising of the delicate limb. Let it be a strict injunction then, to your groom, "Never unscrew the third crutch;"

and if you find the support shifting in its socket, shift the groom as soon as possible, and send the saddle to the saddler to be firmly fixed in.

Why saddlers should fit these supports to turn at all, I can see no good reason. Some men, it is true, say that in putting a lady on horseback it is necessary to turn the third crutch round, so as to prevent it from catching the skirt; but for my own part I could never find any necessity for this, or any difficulty in clearing a lady's skirt when lifting her to the saddle. In purchasing a side-saddle, I repeat, the greatest judgment is necessary as regards the third crutch; while it should be long enough to give a good purchase and be well padded, it should be but *slightly curved*. A crutch that forms a considerable segment of a circle is both inconvenient and dangerous —inconvenient because it is a support of this description (if any) that is in a lady's way in mounting, and dangerous because, if in the hunting field a horse should chance to fall with his fair rider, she would be unable to extricate herself from her fallen steed, inasmuch as the nearly half-circular crutch would completely pin her leg to the horse. It is, in fact, almost as dangerous as if a man were to strap himself to his saddle (which, by the way, I once saw a very determined hunting man do when suffering from weakness in one leg). He had no opportunity, however, of testing his experiment, as the master of the hounds very judiciously told him that, if he persevered, he (the master) would take the hounds home.

Nor is there any possible use in the enveloping of the leg by the thick crutch of the side-saddle. With the slightest possible bend, the support is sufficient if the rider sits fair and true in her saddle, while plenty of stuffing is necessary to avoid bruising the leg, especially in leaping. These "stumpy-looking" third crutches are certainly less sightly in the saddle-room than the more circular ones; but I submit that, inasmuch as it is not seen when the lady is up, it is of more consequence to consult her comfort and safety than the eye of the groom.

When the lady has arranged her dress to her satisfaction, as above described, the next section of the lesson should consist in teaching how she should take up her reins; and here again the greatest care should be taken by the instructor that this is done coolly and *gracefully*, without hurry or "fumbling." A great deal of trouble in this way may be saved by the instructor teaching the lady how to take up her reins on foot. Thus, take an ordinary double bridle, let a lad hold the upper part of the head-stall in one hand, and the bits in the other, and stand opposite the pupil. Hang both reins over your left arm just as they would rest on the neck of the horse, the curb rein underneath, the bridoon rein above. Let the pupil then take hold of *both reins* at the end with the right hand; place the second finger of the left hand between the bridoon reins with the nearside rein uppermost, and the little finger of the same hand between the curb reins, the near-side curb rein uppermost. Let her then place both bridoon and bit reins perfectly flat over the middle joint of the forefinger of the left hand, and drop the end of the reins over the knuckles, then close the thumb firmly down on them. She will find then both bit and bridoon reins equally divided, and an equal facility of causing them to act on the horse's mouth, according to the direction in which she turns the wrist of her left or bridle hand proper, or assists it with her right hand, according to the aids hereafter to be described. The mode of holding the reins above laid down is called in the French school "Mode de Paysanne," or civilian method. The military fashion, which is far more elegant, but not so well adapted at first for a beginner, is as follows.

The pupil takes the end of the bridoon reins between the finger and thumb of the right hand, and passes them over the full of the left, or, to render the explanation still more simple, passes all the fingers of the left hand between them, the off side rein above, and the near side one below; the buckle piece on the knuckle of the forefinger, the rest of the rein hanging loosely down. Let the lady then take the bit or curb reins between the finger and thumb of the right hand, and pass the little finger of the left between them, the near side rein uppermost. With the right hand then let her draw the reins through the left, until—keeping the left hand perfectly quiet—she has a light, almost imperceptible, feeling on the horse's mouth. Let her then turn the bit reins over the middle joint of the forefinger of the left hand, and close the thumb down closely and firmly on them. The reins will then be precisely in the form in which a dragoon's reins are arranged when he is riding a finished horse at a field day or elsewhere. This method is therefore called the "mode militaire." But inasmuch as only a highly-finished horse can be ridden on the bit rein alone by an equally finished rider, in order to assist the latter, and to prevent the horse unduly feeling the action of the curb on his mouth, it is necessary that the rider should draw up the bridoon reins so as to obtain an equal feeling upon both bit and bridoon. Nothing can be more simple than to do this, as the rider has only with the right hand to take hold of the bridoon rein on the left or near side of the buckle or centre, and draw it up until the part passing under the lower edge of the hand is of equal length with the bit reins. She then closes her left thumb on both reins, and shortens the right bridoon rein until it is of equal length with the others. The rider has then an equal feeling of all four reins. She should then hold the ends with her right hand, and let the reins slip through the left until both hands are drawn back close to her waist, the wrists slightly rounded outwards, the back towards the horse's head, and the elbows drawn slightly back behind the waist.

The instructor having placed the pupil's hands, should then proceed to correct her general position. The figure should be well drawn up from the waist, shoulders perfectly square and well thrown back, head and neck erect, the upper part of the arm hanging almost perpendicular from the shoulder, the elbows well back, so that a thin rod would pass between them and the waist; the obvious reason for this position of the hands and elbows being that, if they are allowed to go forward, the whole flexibility of the waist—upon which depends the comfort, grace, and security of the pupil's riding—is destroyed, and the lithe figure of the fair rider becomes rigid and wooden in appearance, and stiff in action.

The upper part of the figure being thus placed, the master's attention should be directed to the position of the feet and legs. That of the right leg I have already described. The left leg, with the knee well bent, should be placed firmly against the third crutch, the heel well sunk, the toe raised from the instep, the foot at first well home in the stirrup. By well stretching down the heel the rider braces all the muscles at the back of the leg, and this, joined to drawing the figure well up from the waist, secures that true balance so indispensable to good riding. The right leg should be well bent and drawn back as near as possible to the left leg.

This should be the position at a walk, the aids for which, and the turns I leave for another chapter.

CHAPTER V.

LET me now offer a few remarks on a subject upon which considerable diversity of opinion exists, namely, whether the teaching of a young lady in riding may or may not be entrusted to a female professor of equitation in preference to a man. At the first glance, there seems to be good reason for preferring the tuition of the lady but, on careful consideration, I believe most of those interested in the matter will agree with me that, under many circumstances likely to occur, one lady, however good a horsewoman herself, is likely to be quite unable to render the desired assistance to a pupil, conceding, at the same time that, as regards the details of dress, the opinion of a lady who has had long practice in the saddle may be very useful.

In the first place, the placing of the pupil on the horse and taking her off cannot possibly be as well done, to say the least, by a lady instructor as it can by a gentleman; neither would the performance of such an office be graceful or convenient to either. Secondly, all that portion of the instruction which should be given by the instructor on foot while the pupil is on horseback can be better given by a man who understands his business than by a lady, because, although the tone of voice in which the instruction is conveyed should be kindly, and the manner cheerful and encouraging, a degree of *firmness* and *conciseness* is necessary, which few ladies possess, for the reason that the art of teaching riding, like riding itself, requires a considerable practice and long drilling into the instructor in a school where smartness of diction and expression form part of the education of an intended professor of equitation. Thirdly, assuming both instructor and pupil to be in the saddle, a lady, although thoroughly mistress of her own horse, is unable to aid her pupil as easily as a man can.

In the early lessons given (the instructor being on horseback), it is necessary that the latter should be close enough to the pupil's horse on the off side to be able at any moment to place the hands of the learner, to check any exuberant action of the horse by laying the left hand firmly upon the reins; and in the first essays made by the pupil in the trotting lesson, to assist her by the left hand of the instructor placed under the right elbow of the beginner.

And finally, should any necessity arise during a ride for dismounting the pupil, a lady instructor labours under this difficulty, that having dismounted herself, and both pupil and teacher being on the ground, the act of mounting again by two ladies, unattended by a man, is one of considerable difficulty and possible danger.

From the very necessity of her position in the saddle, a lady teaching another cannot, without inconvenience to both legs (the left especially), approach near enough to her pupil's horse to assist the latter with her left hand, because her left leg is always in danger of coming in contact with the other horse; while on a windy day the skirt of her habit is likely enough to be blown into his flank, and thereby make him unsteady. Not long since I saw two ladies who were riding, unattended by a man, in a very awkward predicament. Both are practised riders, possessing capital seats and hands, and are equal to any contingency likely to occur as long as they are in the saddle; nay, one of the ladies is, I believe, the most accomplished horsewoman I ever saw. Her seat is both fine and graceful to a degree; her hands perfection, her nerve first-rate, and her experience in riding even difficult horses with hounds considerable. This lady was the elder of the two; her companion was considerably younger, but although a very accomplished rider, she lacked the experience of her friend. Something had gone amiss with the younger lady's saddle, and both ladies dismounted to arrange it. The elder was quite equal to this, for I have seen her many times saddle and bridle her own horse, and with one that would stand quietly (being herself exceedingly supple and active), she can put her hands on the upper pommel and vault into the saddle without any assistance. But in the case I allude to she was completely fixed. Her horse was a chesnut thoroughbred, only four years old; and, although, despite all difficulty I believe, had she been alone, she would have succeeded in mounting, her friend and her horse placed her in an awkward dilemma. She was compelled from time to time to use one hand to disengage the folds of her habit, and she had to hold both horses, even if her friend could have gained her saddle unassisted. Neither horse would stand still; the one, as is invariably the case in such little difficulties, setting a bad example, which the other was not slow to follow. To hold two horses, keep clear of her own habit, while the horses were shifting their positions continually, and give her friend even the least help in mounting, proved too much even for the highly-finished lady equestrian, and as the *contretemps* occurred on a lone country road, I believe they would have been compelled to lead their horses a considerable distance, had I not chanced opportunely to arrive. In such places as Rotten-row a lady instructor may get on tolerably well with her pupil, because, in case of any mishap, there are plenty of men always at hand who know what a horse is; but in out-of-the-way country places it is very different. The British rustic, whatever other good qualities he may possess, is not celebrated, as a rule, for over politeness to ladies—strangers particularly. In proof of the above, there is a story current in this neighbourhood which is likely enough to be true, although I cannot vouch for it myself. The tale runs thus:—A lady (one of the daughters of a noble house) having married, had gone abroad with her husband, and been absent from the home of her early days so long that the uprising generation of young people about the estate knew her not. She was taking a ride one day unattended, and mounted on a steady cob, had been visiting the long-cherished scenes of her childhood, when she came to a very awkward bridle gate, seated on which was a juvenile "wopstraw" in duck frock, leather leggings, and wideawake. The boy jumped down and opened the gate for the lady, at the same time taking off his hat. Now the fair recipient of this delicate attention was well aware of the fact that the village people on the paternal estate were celebrated in the county for their rough manners to strangers, ladies forming no exception, so she was agreeably surprised at the exceptional good behaviour of the youngster, the more so as she was quite sure he did not know her. Taking a shilling out of her purse she gave it to him, observing: "You are a very good boy," and added, laughing, "I am sure you were not born at D." (the name of the principal village on the estate). But to the donor's horror the youngster, grasping his hat firmly in one fist and the shilling in the other, with a fiery glare of indignation in his fat face and flashing eye, replied, "Thou be'st a loyar (liar), I wor."

Verbum sap. All rustics are not so ill behaved as the one above mentioned. But as very few of them will go far out of their road to assist a stranger, it is as well that ladies riding in remote country parts should be attended by a gentleman; and I repeat, for all purposes of instruction, the attendance of a man will be found far more efficient than that of a lady.

CHAPTER VI.

THE frontispiece represents the stamp of horse best calculated to carry a lady, and is a very truthful likeness of a five-year-old horse, named Prince Arthur, a son of the celebrated racehorse Stockwell, his dam a half-bred Arab mare.

The subject of the plate, therefore, has some of the very best English blood in his veins, in conjunction with that Eastern strain from which in all probability our magnificent British thoroughbreds derive a considerable proportion of their power of endurance, or, in turf phraseology, their staying quality.

The horse is a first-class hack, as good a performer over the great Leicestershire pastures and formidable oxers which so often bar the way in that sporting county, as he has already proved himself in the *manége*; and, as he possesses, in addition to true and most elastic action, fine temper and indomitable courage, I venture to present his likeness as my type of the sort of animal adapted either for Rotten-row or to hold his own in the "first flight" over a country.

A common error is that any weedy thoroughbred, too slow for racing, and without the "timber" and substance to enable him to carry a 10-stone man to hounds, is good enough for a lady's riding. There can be no greater mistake. While quality and fashion are indispensable in a woman's horse, strength and substance are equally necessary. As I have before observed, the very conditions upon which the comfort and safety of a lady's riding depend, leave her horse without that support in his action which he would derive from the riding of a good man; while, however true the balance of the lady may be, still the horse's powers are called upon in a long ride, either on the flat or over the country, in a way which tests him severely. There must therefore be plenty of wear and tear in the right place—great strength in the loins, a back *not too short*, aided by strong and well-arched back ribs, which are at the same time not too closely locked up.

The Arab horse proper, despite his great capability of endurance, his symmetrical contour and extraordinary sagacity, is still a trying mount for a lady unaccustomed to him. With great power in his hind quarters (as a rule), he is short in the back, low and short in front of the saddle. The consequence is that from his powerful back action, he pitches too much in his collected paces to ride pleasantly to a woman, although when striding away at top speed he is easy enough.

On the other hand, the English horse that possesses length enough to enable him to travel easily under the fair equestrian too often has the length in the wrong place, and cannot stay—a defect fatal to enjoyable riding for a lady, at all events in the hunting field.

It is to the admixture of Eastern and Western blood, therefore, that one has to look for symmetry of topping conjoined to length in the right place, power, and substance.

I now proceed to say a few words as to the "aids" to be employed to put the horse in motion. In order to impress these thoroughly upon the memory of the fair tyro, the preceptor should adopt a form of question and answer to the following effect:

Q. What are the aids to make a horse walk?—A. A pressure of the leg to his side, at the same time easing the hand.

Q. How is the hand to be eased?—A. From the wrist; the arm being kept perfectly steady, and the little finger yielding towards the horse's neck.

Q. How many lines of action should the little finger of the bridle hand move on?—A. Four. First, towards the waist; second, towards the horse's neck; third, towards the right shoulder; fourth, towards the left.

Q. What are the objects of these motions?—A. First, to collect, halt, or rein back the horse. Second, to give him facility of moving forward. Third, to turn him to the left. Fourth, to turn him to the right. The upper part of the rider's figure to be slightly turned from the waist, by bringing forward the right shoulder when turning to the left and *vice versâ*, in order to enable her to move exactly on the same line as the horse, and so to preserve completely her due *aplomb* or balance in the saddle. The above, in a slightly modified form, is the instruction laid down in the "Military Aid Book," as is the following.

Q. What is meant by a light hand?—A. An almost imperceptible easing and feeling of the bridle hand, so as to preserve the natural delicacy of the horse's mouth.

The foregoing, however, while it indicates correctly and concisely what a light hand is, is scarcely explicit enough for a beginner. I believe the best definition to be this: when a horse is "light in hand," according to the technical meaning, it should by no means be understood that he has so delicate a mouth that he fears the action of the bit in it. On the contrary, having in his breaking been fairly balanced, the greater part of the weight on his haunches, and ridden well up to his bridle, he should admit of a steady *appui* between his mouth and the rider's hand, while he bends in the poll of the neck.

Thoroughly balanced, and bending as above described, his mouth yields to the action of the rider's hand, and is "light" in the true sense of the principles of equitation.

A great deal of nonsense is talked about ladies' hands being so much more light and delicate than those of a man. The truth is, that, assuming both male and female rider to be equally practised in the saddle, there is no difference whatever in the feeling or *appui* given by the horse.

Thoroughly habituated to obey certain indications conveyed to him through the medium of the bridle reins and leg or other aid of the rider, he will answer to them precisely in the same manner to a lady as he would to a man; while, on the other hand, if these indications are not given with well-defined clearness and precision, he will not answer to anybody's riding.

There is a point, however, as regards the action of the hands, to which I beg to call the particular attention both of young ladies commencing their lessons in equitation and of gentlemen (non-professional) who may undertake the task of teaching riding.

A great difference of opinion exists as to whether the action of the bridle hand should be from the wrist only, or whether (spring like, if I may use the expression) the "give and take" action should be conveyed by the upper part of the arm being quite mobile at the shoulder joint and in conjunction with the forearm, the latter kept, however, close to the side, and moving easily and freely to the horse's action. The latter theory is warmly advocated by many thoroughly experienced horsemen and professors of female equitation, who maintain that to teach a young lady to keep the arm firm to the side, in the manner adopted in the military riding school, is not only to give her a rigid wooden appearance on her horse, but also to destroy the proper flexibility of her figure.

On the other hand, some instructors—those especially who are veterans of the cavalry *manége*—insist that firmness of the arm should in all cases be rigidly demanded.

My experience induces me to come to a conclusion which is midway between these opposing theories.

In the first lessons given to a lady on horseback it is well to insist upon her keeping the arm steady, because otherwise she is ready not only to yield her hand to every movement of the horse, be that yielding right or wrong, but gradually and imperceptibly to herself her hands will steal forward until they are eight or ten inches in front of her, the consequence being that the muscles of the waist become rigid, and the flexibility of her figure at its most important point, as regards riding, is lost, while the hands remain in the awkward and ungainly position I allude to.

For the above reason, therefore, it is desirable to inculcate firmness of the lower part of the arm to the side in the early lessons; the hands drawn back close to the waist. And, in order to make this form of riding more easily comprehensible to the pupil at her first essay, the following will be found highly effective:

Let the instructor stand in front of the horse, and taking the bridle reins one in each hand, let him caution the pupil *not* to yield to him if he pulls against her. Let him then take a quick, sharp pull at the reins in the same way as a horse would when trying to get his head free from the rider's control. The master will find that, despite the caution, both the pupil's hands will come forward at once; and if this action on the bridle had been executed by the horse instead of his master, the former would have gained his first step in having his own way, and, for instance, from a collected canter could increase his pace at his own will. Now, there is nothing more important in the action of the hand in controlling the horse than firmness and instantaneous decision in yielding or maintaining the *appui*.

"If" (say some theorists) "a horse pulls against you, drop your hand to him." This is rather a vague expression, which, in fact, conveys no real meaning to an inexperienced person; among horsemen it is intended to convey that you should yield to the horse whenever he pulls or takes a liberty with the hand. Now, the direct reverse of this is the course to be adopted by all riders who wish to acquire good hands. When a horse endeavours to forereach upon the rider, the latter, instead of yielding, should close his hands firmly on the reins, and keep the arms perfectly steady, *without pulling an ounce* against the horse; at the same time closing his leg with equal firmness. In the next stride or two the horse will yield to the hand, which should instantly yield to him; and thus he learns that you are master of him, and goes well together, or, as it is technically called, collectedly and within himself; whereas if the hand is freely yielded whenever he takes a liberty or romps for his head, in a very brief time he will be all abroad, and going in any form but that best for himself or his rider.

To ensure firmness and steadiness of the hands, however, equal firmness and steadiness are requisite in the arms, and, for that reason, the pupil should be taught to keep them close to the side; an additional reason being that, if this is neglected, a beginner, as it were, disconnects the figure from the waist upwards, and loses her true balance. When the pupil has had sufficient practice to ensure steadiness in the saddle, the injunction as to arms perfectly steady may be relaxed; and gradually, while there is no lateral motion of the arm from the side or sticking out of the elbows, the lady will learn to give easy play to the shoulder joint without destroying the neatness of her riding or her power to fix her arms for a moment if the horse tries to get his head away. In short, my theory is that it is impossible for the pupil to learn the true *appui*, or acquire what is usually called a light hand, until she has acquired a steady one. It is easy enough to tell her to "give and take" to the cadence of the horse's action; but the precise moment at which to do this must be made clear to the learner by some well defined and easily comprehensible rule. I submit that the readiest way of defining it is that I have attempted in the foregoing. Having carefully given the above instruction, see that the pupil is sitting fair and true in the saddle, and be careful to correct any tendency to throwing forward the right shoulder, which is both inelegant and destructive of balance. See that the right knee is in a firm, but still flexible form on the upper pannels. Caution the pupil while she draws her figure well up from the waist to stretch the left heel well down; and let her then, keeping her hands perfectly quiet, press the horse forward into a walk with the leg, while she yields the little finger from the wrist only. Let her make the horse walk freely out, but up to his bridle, the whip being applied, if necessary, on the off shoulder if he hangs back behind his work.

Nearly all young people, when first put on horseback, are anxious to be off in a canter at once, and it is a sore trial to their patience to be kept at a walk. But there can be no greater mistake than to allow them to canter a horse until they have learnt the "alpha" of their business—that important lesson, how to make a horse walk true and fair.

This accomplished, "going large" round school or paddock, the pupil should be carefully instructed how to turn her horse square to the right or left, and to rein him back. And in order to make the instruction as clear and concise as possible, again, in a modified form, the "Book of Aids" may be called upon. The formula there laid down, in the shape of question and answer, is as follows:—

Q. How do you turn a horse to the right or left?—A. By a double feeling of the inward rein, retaining a steady feeling of the outward. The horse kept up to the hand by pressure of both legs. The outward by the strongest. Now, as in the case of a lady, there is no right leg to support the horse, in turning, he is liable to lean upon the hand; the rider should close the left leg firmly, and touch him lightly on the off-side with her whip, which will at once cause him to keep his forehand up and his haunches under him. After being once or twice so corrected he will turn carefully, without hurry or coming on his shoulder.

The pupil should then be taught to turn her horse right and left about in the centre of the *manége*, the aids being simply continued until the animal faces the reverse way, the pupil turning her horse upon his centre in the middle of the *manége*, instead of his haunches, as at the side. Plenty of practice should be given in making these turns, because by them the pupil learns to bring up the right or left shoulder according to the hand turned to, the right shoulder in turning to the left, and *vice versâ*; and this should be most carefully attended to by the master, otherwise the body of the pupil is moving on one line and the horse on another, and in case of his flirting the pupil is already half-way out of her saddle. Too much attention therefore cannot be given to this vital point in the *aplomb* for this obvious reason—if a lady once acquires the habit (which unfortunately too many do) of allowing the horse to turn without " going with him." it is quite on the cards that some day a horse, a trifle too fresh, may jump round with her. If the above principle of " going " with the horse has been thoroughly well taught her in her early lessons she will have no difficulty in accompanying the action of the horse, if she even fail in checking it; but if she is permitted so to sit as to be looking over her horse's left ear when she turns him to the right, she is leaving the question of her seat entirely to the generosity of the steed. And it may be as well to say at once that, with the best intentioned, broken, or mannered horse, it may be laid down as a golden rule in riding to leave nothing to his generosity. Horses are very keen in their perceptions, and can detect in a manner little suspected by the inexperienced when they have one at a disadvantage.

Reining back may be practised from time to time. To do this well, again clearly defined instructions should be given. First the horse should be halted. Thus: A light *firm* feeling of both reins, to check his forward movement ; the leg closed tightly at the same time, to keep him up to the hand; the reins to be eased as soon as the horse is halted. The aids for reining back should then be explained as follows : Closing the hands firmly on the reins, the rider should feel the horse's mouth as though the reins were made of silken thread instead of leather, and close her leg quietly to keep him up to the hand. There should be no dead pull at the horse's mouth, but the reins should be eased at every step he takes backwards, which, if the aids are smoothly and truly applied, he will do without throwing his haunches either in or out. In the early lessons the pupil should not be allowed to rein her horse back more than two or three steps at a time. The use of reining back is to bring the greater weight from the horse's forehand to his haunches, to collect him and make him light in hand. (See " Aid Book.") It is also of great use in assisting the pupil to correct her own *aplomb* in the saddle, and acquire a true *appui* on the horse's mouth. Every movement of the hand of the rider, however, and every step of the horse, should be carefully watched by the instructor. The horse should never be allowed to *hurry* back, as that will at once enable him to get behind his bridle.

These lessons at a walk, the turns to the right and left, turns about and reining back, should be continued until the pupil executes them with precision. Her position should be rigidly attended to, all stiffness avoided, and nothing in the shape of careless sitting allowed to pass unnoticed. I repeat, the early lessons should, if anything, be a little overdone in the way of exactness, because any careless habit acquired at such a stage is most difficult to get rid of afterwards. When the pupil is thoroughly *au fait* at her walking lesson, she should commence the next important section, that, namely, of learning to trot, the formula of which I will endeavour to explain in my next chapter, concluding this with a description of the form in which a lady should dismount, and the assistance that should be be afforded by the master.

Having halted the horse in the centre of the school, his head should be held by a steady groom. The lady should then pass the reins from the right hand to the left, and quietly lift her skirt with the right hand until she can easily disengage her right knee from the upper pommels. At the same moment her left foot should be disengaged by the assistant from the stirrup, and her skirt from the near-side pommel or third crutch. The lady should then drop the reins on the horse's neck, and having disengaged her right knee, turn quietly to the left in her saddle, and face the assistant. She should then with both hands take up the slack of her habit until her feet are quite clear of it, otherwise, on alighting she is liable to trip and fall, possibly right into the arms of the assistant, which is not, by any means, according to rule.

Having gathered up the skirt, the lady should then carry her hands forward about eight or ten inches from her knees, and rest both her hands firmly on those of the assistant, who should raise them up well for the purpose. It remains only then for the lady to glide smoothly down from the saddle, and, slightly supported by the assistant, she will alight easily and gracefully on *terra firma*. Some riding masters have a fashion of taking a lady off her horse by placing both hands on her waist and allowing her to throw her weight forward upon them. Such a practice is *outré*, inelegant, and unsafe, because the lady is likely enough to throw more weight forward than the master anticipated, in which case both may come to the ground, to the great discomfiture of the fair equestrian.

CHAPTER VII.

THE TROTTING LESSON.

THIS, once thoroughly mastered, gives the pupil confidence and security on her horse, and is the great inductive step by which she learns the value of balance. Some years ago it was considered that if a lady could sit her horse gracefully at a walk, and securely at a canter, she had accomplished all that was correct or necessary in female equitation. Trotting was altogether ignored, for the simple reason that ladies found it extremely difficult to do, and impossible to find anybody who could help them out of their difficulty by teaching them the right way. In those days most of the riding masters were men who had been instructors in the cavalry. In that arm of the service, trotting according to regulation is quite a different thing to the easy rise and fall seat practised by civilians on horseback. It is a necessity in cavalry, in order to preserve the dressing in line, that a man should sit down in his saddle at a trot, and allow the horse to shake him fair up and down in it. If the rising seat were allowed, it would be impossible to preserve anything like dressing. This shake-up, or "bumping" seat, however, as men out of the army call it, is by no means so distressing as some people imagine, unless the horse is unusually rough in his action.

The reason is that the military trot is taught upon the principle of balance. The man sits fair down on his seat, and, keeping his knee forward and his heel well down, does not cling to the horse by muscular grasp; consequently the bumping, so terrific to the eye of the civilian, is scarcely felt by the soldier, and in continental armies, where rough trotting horses are exceptional, the motion or jolt is scarcely perceptible. There are a great many popular fallacies about military riding—as, for instance, that a dragoon rides with a very long stirrup; that his seat is insecure; that the bumping gives a horse a sore back; and that, except a sailor and a tailor, a dragoon officer is about the worst horseman to be found. This is not exactly the place to enter into any controversy on the subject; but I may as well observe at once, and I do so because I am sure the old soldiers are not altogether despised by the ladies, even in this non-military country, that all the foregoing are so many mistakes. A dragoon, any time within my memory, rode just the same length as a man does over a country—that is to say that, measuring the cavalry man's leather and iron by the length of his arm and hand, which is the right length for a civilian, you have exactly the cavalry regulation length. The stirrup of a lancer indeed is somewhat shorter than that used by most hunting men. Finally, an acquaintance with the *habitués* of such places as Melton would prove to unbelievers in the riding of cavalry officers that the names of most of the men who go to the front in the hunting-field, and keep there, are to be found in the " Army List." I have been tempted thus to digress by having referred to the military riding school, from which in former days, most, if not all, the riding masters who taught ladies came. Now, although I stand up (as in duty bound) for the military system of riding *per se*, it does not produce the right man to teach a woman to ride, if the experience of the preceptor has been acquired in the riding school only. Excellent as is our system (or, rather, the German system, for it is imported from the Prussian service), for making a man a first-class dragoon, as regards anything connected with a lady's seat or the principle of her balance, it is useless.

As regards her hands, or the application of the "aids" of the *manège*, it is highly beneficial, because nothing can be more clear or concise than the simple rules laid down in military equitation for the application of the "helps," by which a horse's easy movement is controlled and regulated. It was principally to the want of men who could teach a lady to ride, however, that the absence of a trotting in the side saddle was to be attributed " lang syne."

It is altogether different now. Riding masters took to riding across country, and their daughters took to it also, naturally.

Awkward spills occurred; and long journeys home after hunting, all done at a canter, terribly shook the horse's legs and the temper of the head of the family. " Why the deuce can't you let your horse trot?" I once heard the worthy sire of a blooming girl of sixteen say to his daughter, who was pounding away on the hard road on the *retour de chasse.* " For God's sake let him trot, Carry. You'll hammer his legs all to pieces. Why don't you let him trot?' " Because, pa, he won't let me trot," was the unanswerable reply. True enough; Carry knew nothing about it, and there was nobody to tell her. She was riding on a saddle that fitted neither her nor her horse. She had no third crutch, and she had a slipper stirrup (that worst of abominations in ladies' saddlery). Looking back at those days, the only wonder to me is, how ladies managed to ride at all. That they did ride is certainly proof (if any were wanting) of their courage and perseverance under difficulties.

The necessity for trotting having become apparent as ladies took more to riding, it at length called the attention of one or two thoroughly practical men to the subject. The first of these, I believe, was the celebrated steeple race jockey, Dan Seffert, who had been a riding master in his early days, and who was equally at home in the *manége* or between the flags over a country.

The running made by Mr. Seffert was soon taken up by other first-class horsemen, among whom were Mr. Oldacre, and Mr. Allen, of Seymour-place. The third crutch was added to the side saddle, and numerous improvements effected in it, which rendered trotting not only practicable, but pleasant and easy to a lady, provided she was taught the right way. I believe we owe the third crutch and padded stirrup to Mr. Oldacre, a first-class judge of female equitation ; but I am not quite certain upon this point. The saddle having been rendered practicable for the purpose, the next thing requisite was a comprehensible and simple set of rules, by which the lady could be taught to trot, without distressing either her horse or herself. To whom these rules owe their origin is immaterial; as to their efficiency, such as they are, I have found them highly so, and therefore beg leave to submit them to your readers.

After the usual walking lesson (abridged, however, to allow more time for what is to follow), the pupil should ride her horse to the centre of the school, and halt him there, so that the instructor has perfect facility of getting at the horse on any side, and seeing the exact form in which his pupil moves. The lady should then be instructed to take a firm hold with the right knee on the upper pommel of the saddle, grasping it well between the thigh and the lower part of the leg, and carrying the latter well back, with the heel sunk as close as possible to the left leg. By sinking the heel well, she will give great firmness to her hold with the right leg upon the upper pommels. To accomplish this, however, she should get well forward in her saddle, and care should be taken that her stirrup is not too short, otherwise she will be thrown too far back to enable her to take the necessary grip with the upper leg. The left leg should then be well drawn back, the front of the thigh pressed firmly against the third crutch, the left heel well sunk, and the toe raised from the instep, because a firmness is thus given to the leg and thigh which would otherwise be wanting. The body, from the waist upwards, should be inclined slightly forward, and the angle at which the left foot is drawn back from the perpendicular line from the knee to the foot should be regulated by the inclination of the body forward, so as exactly to balance it.

Having placed his pupil in this position, and seen that her hands are well drawn back and arms firm, the instructor should then *take her foot out of the stirrup*, and give the following concise instructions : " On the word ' one,' raise the body slowly from the saddle as high as possible." Now, to do this without the aid of the stirrup can only be accomplished by keeping the heel well down and the leg back (in the first place, in order to balance the body), and then raising the figure by the action of the right knee and its grasp upon the upper pommel. At first the pupil will find this difficult, even when the horse is perfectly motionless, and when the riding master assists her by putting his left hand under her left elbow ; but after a few efforts she will succeed. This is the first step in learning the rise with precision. Having accomplished it, the pupil should not lower herself again to the saddle until the instructor gives her the word "two," when she should lower herself as slowly as she rose.

If she has been well tutored in the extension and suppling practices alluded to in my second chapter, she will understand what "one, two" time means in this way as well as in dancing, and her knowledge of balance on foot will assist her on horseback. These rising and falling motions should be continued until the pupil executes them with precision, fair intervals of rest being allowed. The master should then place the lady's foot again in the stirrup.

The absence of this support in the previous lesson will have prevented the pupil from leaning to the near side, and throwing her weight out of the perpendicular—a most pernicious habit, which ladies who try to learn their trotting in one lesson are very apt to fall into, and it is a fault very difficult to correct. In fact, the main object in beginning without a stirrup is to avoid this error.

With the support of the stirrup the pupil will find the act of rising and maintaining an upright or slightly bent forward position (the figure raised well up from the saddle) a comparatively easy matter, and the lesson should be continued thus for a quarter of an hour longer. However trying to the patience this riding without gaining ground—"marking time" in the saddle—may be, the lady may be assured, that it is by rigid attention to such minutiæ only that she can become a first-class horsewoman, and that she is in reality losing no time.

When we hear the singing of Mme. Titiens, or recollect the unrivalled dancing of Taglioni, we are apt to forget that with all the natural talent of these great artistes, it was close attention to rudimentary elements that laid the foundations of their excellence. It is so in riding, to excel in which is far more difficult than in dancing. It is those only who are content with mediocrity who ignore detail. We come now to the second section of this lesson, in which the pupil will begin to find the first fruit of her previous exertion. The master having led her horse to the side of the school, should give her instruction to walk him freely out, riding him, however, well up against the snaffle, if necessary for this purpose using her whip sharply. The horse will then take fairly hold of her hand, and give her a good *appui*. The rising and falling should then be continued at a walk, and assisted by the impetus given by the horse's forward motion, and the stirrup, the pupil will find her work still easier than when the horse was at a standstill.

The instructor should now count his "one," "two," in different times, allowing a longer or shorter interval between each word, according to whether he means to convey to the pupil the notion of quick sharp action in the horse, or long dwelling action. Thus, when the horse trots, he will be able to count his time in exact accordance with the animal's movements. Be the time quick or slow that he counts, he should exact rigid conformity of action in the pupil; because this harmony of motion to the counting is as important to success in the riding master as it is to the music master. Time and cadence in action are vital points in equitation.

As soon as the instructor is satisfied that his pupil can easily accommodate her action to his word, he should prepare to test both in the trot. But if he takes a week to get the pupil to do the two previous lessons (one of them even) properly, they should be continued until she does it; nobody can spell until he knows the alphabet.

To carry on the lesson in the trot, the instructor should mount a cob or pony of such height as will admit of his easily placing his left hand under the right elbow of the pupil. He should ride with his reins in his right hand, and be sure that the horse he gets on is a perfectly steady one.

He should now put plenty of vivacity into his own manner; he will then easily impart it to his pupil and her horse. The latter should be smartly "woke up" if at all behind his work—pressed up to the bridle with whip and leg, and "made ready" to increase his pace at any moment. The master should then caution his pupil that on the words "Prepare to trot," she should strengthen her grasp on the upper pommel, her pressure against the third crutch, and well stretch down the left heel, while she carries back the left leg, and inclines the body slightly forward from the waist, arms very firm, fingers shut tight on the reins; and while the body inclines forward there should be no outward or lateral curvature of the spine, nor should the head be dropped. The shoulders pressed well back, and the hands close to the waist, will give firmness and suppleness to the whole figure. Directly the master is satisfied with the pupil's position, he should place his left hand under her right elbow, urge his own horse smartly on, and give the word "Trot," on which the pupil should, without altering her position or yielding her hand, touch her horse smartly on the shoulder with the whip; he will then trot forward. At the first step he takes the master should help the pupil up with his left hand, and commence counting his "one," "two" in exact accordance with the horse's action. In nine cases out of ten the lady will succeed, with a fair stepping horse, in catching at the first attempt the rise at the right moment, and the increased impetus given by the horse will assist her, while her preparatory lessons in rising and falling will now prove their value.

Should any failure, however, attend the first effort, both horses should again be brought to the walk; the lady should be allowed to re-arrange her habit, and recover from the inevitable flurry which attends any failure of this sort. Patience, concise explanation, and cheerful manner on the part of the master will presently find their reward. All ladies do not possess great nerve, but most of them have great courage and perseverance, and after a false start or two they get on their mettle, and are sure to catch the true action. When once they have it, the master should make the pace sharp and active three or four times round the school, which is long enough for a first attempt. A couple more turns of equal duration should terminate the first trotting lesson. The lady should walk her horse round the school until both are cool, make much of him by patting him on the neck, and then be taken off. Day by day the instructor can slightly increase the length of the lesson, always beginning it, however, as above described, until the rise and fall of the pupil at a trot is perfectly true and fair. There should be no twist from the waist, the shoulders perfectly square, every movement in exact harmony with the horse's action. After the lady can rise and fall in the saddle unaided by the master, he is better on foot, because he can stand behind his pupil, and at once correct any fault in her position or riding; and no fault, be it remembered, however trivial, should be allowed to pass uncorrected.

For some time the lady should continue trotting out round the school, riding altogether upon the snaffle and sending her horse well up against it. There should be no "give-and-take" action in the hand in this case; but while she does not pull the weight of a feather against her horse, she should make him maintain the *appui* by taking well hold of her hand; his trot will then be regular and fair.

After about ten days or a fortnight of such practice, the master may commence the third section of his trotting lesson, namely, that in which the pupil begins to collect her horse, raise his forehand, and bring his haunches under him.

The first step in this should be to ascertain that the lady is not dependent upon the horse's mouth for any part of her firmness in the saddle, or, more correctly speaking, to see that her balance is right unaided by the bridle, because, although perhaps imperceptible to the rider (man or woman), the *appui* of the mouth has more to do with the seat than most people imagine. In good schools of equitation men tell you "There are no hands without legs." True, and if we were to ask many a good man that we see crossing a country to ride over a big fence without a bridle we should perceive that there are few seats without hands. It is to correct the tendency to trust for support to the horse's mouth that the efforts of the instructor should now be directed.

To carry this out, he should be mounted upon a horse of about equal height to that of his pupil, on the off side, and close to whom he should place himself. He should direct her to drop her reins entirely, and then take them in his left hand, riding his own horse with his right. He should then instruct the lady to place her hands behind her waist, the right hand grasping the left elbow, as described in the suppling practices. Cautioning her again as to firmness of grasp and good balance, he should then urge both horses into a smart trot, and keep them going round the school two or three times, carefully watching the action of the pupil, and if he perceives the least indication of distress pull up immediately. The exertion necessary to execute this lesson is severe if the pupil has not been well suppled before being put on horseback. If she has, there will be considerably less effort in it; but, in any case, on first practising it, the fair tyro requires every encouragement to persevere, because in doing one thing well, she is very apt to forget another. Constantly reminded as to her position as the trot goes on, she will succeed in doing all well. After two or three such turns (the arms of course disengaged during the interval), the lady should take up her reins again; this time the curb and snaffle reins of equal length, and in the form (No. 1) described in a previous chapter. She should then trot her horse freely out round the school, and she will find the full benefit of her recent drilling without reins, inasmuch as her seat will be many degrees firmer, and her balance more true, leaving her more liberty of action in hand and leg to apply the necessary aids to her horse in the coming lesson, in which at a well-regulated and collected pace, she will learn to turn him in any direction at her will, to rein him back, to make the inclines and circles, and prepare him for the cantering lesson by finally riding him in his trot entirely on the curb rein, and throwing him well upon his haunches.

CHAPTER VIII.

THE TROTTING LESSON (*continued*).

I COME now to the final section of the trotting lesson—that which, thoroughly acquired, I may term the thorough bass of the matter. Having satisfied himself that his pupil has command of her horse, steady seat and hands, and true balance when riding equally on the snaffle and curb, the master should proceed to instruct her as to the mode of arranging the reins so as to ride on the curb alone.

As this has been already described, it is needless to repeat the formula. I may observe, however, that, in order to give increased facility of action to the bridle hand, and avoid anything like sudden jerk or rough pull upon the horse's mouth, it is best for the lady to retain the end of the curb reins between the fore finger and thumb of her right hand, by doing which she is enabled, keeping her left hand perfectly steady, and opening and closing the fingers, to give easy play to the reins. Without this she would find riding on the curb alone difficult at first with the left hand only, because all the motion must come from the wrist, and considerable practice is necessary to accommodate this motion exactly to the action of the horse. Care should be taken that the elbows are kept well back, so as to preserve the suppleness of the waist, and by this time also the pupil ought to have acquired sufficient steadiness in the saddle to admit of her giving easy play to the upper part of the arm at the shoulder joint. But until complete firmness of seat is gained this should not be attempted, because in the case of a novice it disconnects the figure, and interferes with the horse's mouth materially. The most rigid attention also should be given to the pupil's

THE BARB AND THE BRIDLE.

general position, and the firmness and correct placing of both legs—the heels well down, the upper part of the body well drawn up from the waist, "the whole figure pliant and accompanying every movement of the horse" (see "Military Aid Book").

The lady should commence the lesson by walking her horse two or three times round the school; and it is here, by close attention, that she will learn that light hands are neither "heaven-born" nor impossible to acquire. On pressing the horse forward with her leg or whip, so as to make him walk up against the curb, it is possible her hand may be a little heavy, and that the horse may resist it. In this case, if not cautious and carefully watched, she will let her hands go forward. It is for the instructor to take special care of this, and point out to his pupil how she can ease the reins through her left hand by the aid of the right, so as to catch the true *appui*, without yielding altogether to the horse. In other words, she should allow sufficient rein to go through her hand to enable the horse to walk freely forward; and then, closing her fingers again firmly, make him go up to every hair's breadth of rein she has given him, and fairly against the curb. There should not be a particle of slack rein. In fact, it may be received as a sound principle in riding that there should never be slack reins, no matter what the pace. If you give your horse the full length of the reins even, make him go up to them.

When once the lady has gained the above-named *appui* (the right hand assisting the left), she should be instructed to halt her horse lightly on his haunches preparatory to reining back. And again she should do this by drawing the reins through the fingers of her left hand with the right, keeping the former perfectly steady, and drawing her own figure well up, in order to avoid any tendency to lean forward. On the word "Rein back," which should be given in a very quiet tone of voice, and in the exact cadence in which the master desires his pupil to move her horse to the rear, the lady should feel both reins lightly but firmly for a moment, closing at the same instant her leg so as to keep her horse's haunches under him, in the manner before described when using the snaffle only, but in the present case with greater care and precision. *Lightly* and *firmly* feeling the curb reins while pressed by the leg, the horse will take a step back. The reins should be yielded the instant he does so. Two or three steps back are sufficient, when the word "Forward" should be given, preceded by the caution to close the fingers firmly on the reins, and, with whip and leg, keep the horse well up to his work. Feeling this amount of constraint laid upon him, the horse will be inclined at any moment to canter. But here the tact of the master should be exhibited in instructing his pupil to release the horse from his fore-shortened position, by allowing about six inches of rein (or more, if necessary), to pass through her left hand as she presses the horse forward into a free trot (about eight miles an hour). All her firmness of seat will be necessary now, because any irregular action on her part will cause her hand to become heavy, and make the horse canter. The great thing is, not to continue trotting on the curb-rein alone too long. Short lessons often repeated, and intervals in which to correct everything are best for pupil and instructor.

When the lady can accomplish trotting out for twenty minutes without allowing her horse to break, she should then be instructed to collect him to a slower pace, bringing him more upon his haunches, and with his forehand more up. This requires the nicest tact and discrimination on the part of the rider, perfect steadiness in the saddle, and firm pressure of the left leg; while the reins should be drawn through the left hand with as much care as though the lady feared to break them. The shortened pace should be smart and active, and the horse so collected as to be ready to turn to the right, or left, or about, or make the inclines at any moment. All these exercises should then be practised in the same order as when the pupil rode, assisted by or on the snaffle only.

After the lady has performed these to the satisfaction of the master, she should bring her horse to the walk and be instructed to carry the end of the curb reins, which she has held hitherto in her right hand, through the full of the left hand, and place both reins (the off-side one uppermost) over the middle joint of the fore finger, and close the thumb firmly on them. The end of the reins should be dropped to the off-side of the horse, and hang down outside the off-side crutch; the whip (with the point *downwards*) kept quiet.

Raising the point of the whip, when a lady is trotting a horse on the curb alone, and unassisted by her right hand, is very apt to make him break, because the point of the whip is always in motion, and causes the horse to turn his eye back at it.

The instructor should now carefully place the lady's bridle hand, with the wrist rounded outwards and the thumb pointing square across the body, the back of the hand towards the horse's head, and the little finger turned upwards and inwards towards the waist, the arm perfectly firm, and the wrist quite supple—as in this case it is from the wrist only that every indication to turn, to halt, or rein back is given, aided by the whip on the off side and the leg on the near side. The pupil can then be taught to turn her horse to either hand, or about, at a walk, without any motion of the bridle hand perceptible to a looker-on, although perceptible enough to the horse. In turning to the right, the little finger should be turned down towards the left shoulder, and the back of the hand turned up. This movement will shorten the right rein, and cause it to act on the right jaw of the bit. The whip should be closed firmly (not with a blow) just behind the flap of the saddle on the off side. The left leg supporting this will cause the horse to turn square to his right. Exactly the reverse movement will turn him to the left. Right or left about, aids continued, until the horse has reversed his front.

The trotting lesson may then be gone through again, the pupil riding entirely with the left hand. But in beginning these lessons care should be taken to let them be very short, because, in spite of all previous supplying, considerable constraint is thrown upon the wrist at first. Any yielding to the horse is accomplished by turning the little finger towards his neck, while to collect him simply the little finger is turned up again towards the waist. But the fingers and thumb of the bridle hand must be kept firmly shut upon the reins, otherwise the hand becomes heavy and uneven in its action.

By lessons, gradually increased in length, the pupil should be accustomed thus to ride her horse throughout the trotting lesson, and trot him out, riding with one hand. It is not usual for ladies to continue for any length of time riding in this form; but it is highly necessary that they should be thoroughly well practised at it, otherwise an important part of their course of equitation will be neglected. The same may be said of the bending lesson, previous to cantering. It is rarely put in practice by any but professional female equestrians. But a lady ought to be thoroughly acquainted with its formula, because it teaches the principle upon which a horse acquires his *souplesse*, which is just as necessary to his freedom of action and pleasant riding as the early suppling lessons of the pupil herself were conducive to her own progress.

CHAPTER IX.

The Bending and Cantering Lesson.

According to the ordinary acceptation of the term, a horse is supposed "to bend well" when he arches his neck, yields to the bit, and uses his knees and hocks freely. This alone by no means conveys an adequate idea, however, of what is meant by bending a horse in the scientific sense. The "Military Aid Book" supplies the following question and answer, which gives in a very concise form a better notion of the matter.

Question: What is the use of the "bending lesson"?—Answer: To make the horse supple in the *neck* and *ribs*, to give free action to his shoulder, and teach him to obey the pressure of the leg.

It will be seen, then, that "bending a horse" really means rendering him supple in every portion of his frame, and especially in his ribs and intercostal muscles, as it is suppleness in that part that gives him the lithe, easy motions so pleasant to the rider.

I have before observed that I do not consider an intimate knowledge of the "haut école de manége" indispensable for ordinary riding purposes, either for a lady or gentleman. But, although the "bending lesson" thoroughly carried out may be said to be the very gist of "*haut école* riding," even in its *simple form*, unaccompanied by the higher aids, it is of great service in rendering a horse docile and obedient to hand and leg, and for that purpose is always resorted to in our schools of military equitation.

Now, although I do not expect every lady to acquire the art of suppling her own horses, still a knowledge of the "bending lesson" will make her thoroughly acquainted with the reasons why a horse renders ready obedience to her aids of hand and leg; and, on the contrary, why he resists them.

Stiffness (as it is technically termed) has more to do with what is commonly called restiveness than most people imagine. A horse is asked to do something that calls upon him to bend or supple a joint in which, even in early youth, he is still far from supple. He cannot do it. The rider perseveres, and the horse resists. Whereas, when he is thoroughly suppled, he does not know how to disobey his rider (supposing the latter to know what he is about). If a lady, therefore, will pay close attention to the instruction of her master, she will discover that her horse will obey her more readily, and move with more ease to himself and her, when she applies her aids "smoothly" (without which the bending lesson cannot be done), than by the application of sudden or violent indications of her will. For it must be borne in mind that a double bridle is an instrument of great power in a horse's mouth, and that what may seem light handling to the uninitiated rider may be rough to the horse. A fair amount of practice, therefore, in the above-named exercise will have the effect of rendering a lady's hands remarkably true and steady; and, although the lesson may be a little trying to the patience, the pupil will find her reward in increased confidence and proficiency.

For all practical purposes the "bending lesson" proper may be divided into two sections, namely, the "passage" and the "shoulder in," all other movements of the lesson being simply variations from the above named. The "half passage" may be looked upon as an introduction to the "full passage," but admits of being practised with facility at an increased pace at the trot or canter, and at the latter is a very elegant exercise. To begin with the "shoulder in." Let us suppose a horse standing parallel to the boards at the side of the school. To place him in the desired position it is necessary to bring his forehand in, so that his fore and hind legs are placed upon two lines, parallel to each other and to the boards, and then to bend his head inwards at the poll of the neck. No more correct idea, I believe, can be conveyed of the position than that given in the "Aid Book," which furnishes the following answer to the question, How should a horse be placed in "shoulder in"? "Ans.: When a horse is properly bent in 'shoulder in,' the whole body from head to croup is curved; the shoulders leading, fore and hind feet moving on two lines parallel to each other, hind feet one yard from the boards."

Again. "Q. What are the aids for working this lesson?—A. On the word 'right or left shoulder in,' the horse's forehand is brought in by a double feeling of the inward rein, the outward leg closed, so as to bring the horse's hind feet one yard from the boards."

The outward rein leads, the inward preserves the bend; a pressure of the inward leg (of the rider) compels the horse to cross his legs; the outward leg keeps him up to the hand and prevents him from swerving. The horse should be well bent in the pole of the neck, and well kept up to the hand with the outward leg, the shoulders always leading.

It will be seen from the above that the rider compels, or rather *coaxes*, the horse, by very firm and steady aids, to move with his forehand well up, and his whole figure bent (neck and ribs), with his feet moving on two distinct parallel lines—the effect being to call upon every important joint, and thoroughly to supple the ligaments and tendons, as well as to create muscular development, in a way similar to that of gymnastic or extension exercises in the human being. With young horses in training it is necessary to watch this lesson very carefully, and never to "ask too much" at one time, because any forcing of it would certainly result in restiveness; the strain, even with naturally supple horses, is considerable, and must not be persevered with one moment after it is eivdently painful. Of course, in the case of a lady practising the lesson, it must be done upon a horse that has gone through a long course of teaching, and to whom, therefore, the movements cause no inconvenience. But even here the pupil will find that she must use her hand and leg with firmness, steadiness, and decision, without hurry or impatience, or the horse will not answer to her.

The movement must be executed very slowly, and at first only by a few steps at a time, because, however *au fait* at his work the horse may be, the pupil will find considerable difficulty in continuing to apply the aids.

In working the "shoulder in" to the right, it is necessary for the master, after putting the horse and rider in true position, to place himself on the horse's off side, when he should give the word, "Right shoulder in—march!" The lady then, firmly closing her left leg to keep the horse up to the hand, should keep her right hand well back and low down close to the saddle, lead the horse off with the left rein, and close her whip to his ribs on the off side, just behind the flap of the saddle.

If the horse has been accustomed to work the lesson, with a lady he will obey these aids. But in some cases it is necessary for the master (to supply the absence of the right leg of a man to the horse), to push firmly with his left hand against the horse's ribs to move him off. The rider, while leading the horse off with the left rein, should keep up a continual, light easy play of the right rein, so as to preserve the bend inwards. The instructor should count "one, two," in very slow time, as the horse moves first his fore and then his hind leg. After a few steps onward the horse should be halted, by the rider feeling both reins, and closing the whip firmly on the off side. He should then be made much of and moved on again. A quarter of an hour is ample for the first lesson.

After the pupil understands and can apply the aids for the "shoulder in" (riding on the snaffle), she may be taught to do it on snaffle and curb together, and then on the curb alone, when she will find the nicest balance in her seat and the most careful and delicate manipulations of the reins necessary—joined, however, to distinct and perceptible feeling upon the horse's mouth. And on moving her horse forward she will find that her hand is true and steady.

The "shoulder in" having been neatly done, the lady should rein her horse lightly back and ride him forward, *making the corner* of the school quite square, and then halt at the centre marker. On the word "right half passage," she should turn the horse's head square down the centre of the school, and exactly reverse the aids by which she worked the "shoulder in"; that is, she should lead the horse off with the right or inward rein, well balancing and assisting its power by the outward one; with her leg she should press the horse until he places one foot before the other, gaining ground to his front, and obliquely to his right at the same time, until he arrives at the boards, when he will completely have changed the hand he was working to, and at a canter would, if necessary, be called upon to strike off with the left leg instead of the right.

After executing the "half passage" correctly, the pupil may practise the "full passage," the difference between which and the "shoulder in" is again concisely explained in the "Aid Book."

"Q. What is the difference between the 'passage' and 'shoulder in'?—A. In the passage the horse bends and looks the way he is going. The outward are crossing over the inward legs, and the inward rein leads. In the 'shoulder in' the horse does not look the way he is going. The inward are crossing over the outward legs, and the outward rein leads."

"Q. What is the difference between the full and half passage?—A. In the 'full passage' the horse crosses his legs. In the 'half passage' he only half crosses them, placing one foot before the other."

The pupil will find the passage much more easy to execute than the "shoulder in," though, I repeat, no horse would do the former up to the hand as he ought to do unless he has been well drilled in the latter.

The greatest care on the part of both master and pupil is indispensable to carry out this lesson. The slightest inadvertence or false movement is at once answered on the part of the horse by his taking advantage of it and putting himself in a wrong position, whereas if he is carefully ridden, and kept well up to the hand, the subsequent cantering lesson will be much more easy to perform.

It must be clearly understood, however, that for a lady to attempt to execute the "bending lesson" by written directions alone, and unaided by the vigilant superintendence and oral instruction of a first-rate master would be a mistake. Clear and concise as the language of the "Aid Book" is, it is impossible for any man writing such directions to indicate the precise moment at which each movement of hand and leg is to be made, any more than the man who writes the score in music can regulate the hand of the instrumental executant of it. There must be energy, patience, and close attention on the part of the pupil; vigilance, patience, temper, and thorough knowledge of his craft on the part of the instructor. Master and pupil thus in accord, the latter will derive great advantage and insight into the elegant accomplishment she is endeavouring to acquire, while anything like carelessness on either side will be fatal to the utility of the lesson. It should be thoroughly well done or not at all.

After the careful execution of the above lesson, the pupil should prepare her horse for cantering by reigning him back lightly on his haunches; touching him if necessary smartly with her whip, in order to put him well up to his work. A step or two back (*well up to the bridle*) is sufficient, when she should move forward, and the instructor should give her the aids for cantering; which (once more to quote the simple language of the "Aid Book") are as follows: "A light firm feeling of *both* reins to raise the horse's forehand, a pressure of both legs to keep his haunches under him, a double feeling of the inward rein, and a stronger pressure of the outward leg, will compel the horse to strike off true and united."

The above of course is intended as instruction to a man; but substituting a light tap of the whip on the off shoulder for the pressure of the inward leg of the man, and very light for strong aids, the instruction holds good in the case of the lady.

Now, I have observed before that a horse to be thoroughly broken to carry a woman should be taught to answer to very light aids, and require, in fact, very little leg in order to understand and answer to the indications of his rider's will. If this has been properly carried out the lady will have no difficulty in striking her horse off to the right, *true and united*, which means in cantering to the right (as nearly every hack and lady's horse does) with the off fore, followed by the off hind leg.

A charger or "high *manége*" horse—which must use either leg with equal facility, and go to the left as well as the right—in cantering to the former hand will go with the near fore, followed by the near hind, and be still "true and united" in his pace.

When he goes with the near fore, followed by the off hind, or *vice versâ*, he is "disunited."

A point of vital importance to be looked to by the master is that his pupil at her first attempt at cantering her horse is perfectly cool and self-possessed, and that she applies her aids *smoothly*, without hurry or excitement, for so great is the sympathy of the horse in this respect, that flurry on the part of the rider is sure to cause passionate, excited action in the horse. The manner of the master has much to do with this; while it should be such as to keep his pupil and her horse *eif* and on their metal, he should be careful not to crowd the former with too much instruction at once. Her position should be corrected before she is allowed to strike her horse off. Care should be taken that her arms are firm, and hands well back. The waist should be bent slightly forward, which will give it more suppleness. She should have a firm grip of the upper crutches, both heels well down, and at her first effort she should ride equally upon the snaffle and curb reins. To do this (assuming that she is riding with her bridle in military form), it is only necessary that she should draw up the slack of the near-side snaffle rein with her right hand until it is level with and under the near-side curb rein; then carry the snaffle rein thus shortened over the middle joint of the forefinger of the left hand, and shut the thumb firmly on them. She can then place the slack of the off-side snaffle rein for a moment under the left thumb, while she places the rein between the third and little finger of the right hand, brings the rein through the full of the hand over the middle joint of the forefinger, and closes the thumb firmly on it. The whip should be held in the full of the hand, the point downwards.

With her hands and figure in the above-named form, the lightest application of the aids ought to strike her horse off "true and united;" but if by any chance he takes off with the wrong leg or "disunited," as may sometimes happen with the best broken horse, from a little over-eagerness or anxiety on the part of the pupil, or a little unsteadiness of hand, the master should cause her to bring her horse again to the walk, and reassure her—taking care, however, on these occasions that she never "makes much of" or caresses her horse, which would tend to confirm him in a bad habit, but reins him back, and again puts him up to his bridle.

It is a rare occurrence when a horse (thoroughly well-broken) strikes off incorrectly; but I am endeavouring to write for every contingency.

Assuming the horse to have struck off smoothly to the instructor's word *Ca-a-n-te-r*—which should be given in a quiet, soothing tone of voice, and drawn out as if every letter were a syllable—the horse should be allowed to canter freely forward, although without rush or hurry. The pace should not be too collected at first; the military pace of manœuvre is about the correct thing; eight miles an hour or thereabouts; the cadence true; the horse well ridden into his bridle, and in this case *yielding to the bit*—because, in cantering, it is necessary to have an *appui* upon the mouth, quite different from that to be maintained in trotting, in which it is best for the lady that the horse should feel her hand fairly and firmly, and that there should be little " give-and-take " action of the latter. In cantering, on the other hand, an easy give-and-take play of the hands is indispensable, to cause the horse to bend in the poll of his neck, yield to the hand, and go in true form. By this time the pupil should have acquired sufficient firmness and *aplomb* in the saddle to justify the instructor in commencing to impart to her that mobile action and flexibility of the upper arm at the shoulder joint, which may be regarded as the artistic finishing of her course of equitation. But it will not do to commence this (so goes my experience) at the outset of the cantering lesson, wherein at first it is best to insist upon firmness of the arms, otherwise the pupil is most likely (imperceptibly to herself) to allow her hands to glide forward, and thus destroy the flexibility of her waist, which is a point always to be most carefully watched. It is possible that at first the figure of the pupil, from over-anxiety to maintain her position and ride her horse correctly at the same time, may be somewhat rigid; but complete flexibility cannot be expected at once. It must be remembered that, although the action of cantering in a horse is much easier than trotting, still it is novel to the rider, who moreover has to keep her horse up to his work.

THE BARB AND THE BRIDLE.

It is not the case of putting a young lady upon an old tittuping hack that can do little else than canter along behind the bridle and "drag his toe" at a walk. A horse that has any action or quality in him, and has been taught to trot up to his bridle, requires "asking" to canter, and in the early efforts of the pupil requires keeping to his work a little after he has struck off in his canter, otherwise he will drop into a trot again. Such a horse, however, is the only one upon which to teach a lady to ride. The easy-going old hack above alluded to is fit only for an invalid to take the air on. At the same time it is asking a good deal from the pupil in her early cantering lessons to keep her horse up to his work, and to maintain her own position correctly; and if she exhibits a little stiffness or formality (if I may use the expression) at first, it may fairly be passed over until increased confidence permits the master to give his attention to what I may perhaps call the "unbending" of his pupil. After a few days' cantering as above described, the lady may begin to collect her horse; and by this time also she should be fitted with a spur, of which the best I know is Latchford's patent. An opening in the skirt on the inside is necessary. The shank of the spur should not be too short, otherwise it is very apt to cut holes in the habit. The pupil, when the spur is first fitted on, should be cautioned to keep her left toe as near the horse's side as the heel, in order to avoid hitting him when he does not require it; and, indeed, the wearing of the steel aid is in itself a good exercise as to the true position of the left leg, while the blunt head of a Latchford (when not pressed hard to the horse's side) does away with any danger.

The use of the spur in a lady's riding is objected to by some; but I cannot consider any rider (man or woman) worthy of the name who cannot use one and be safe enough in the saddle at the same time. One objection to spurs for ladies is, that they are apt to do all sorts of mischief in the event of the lady being thrown from her horse. Now, the latter is a contingency which (except in the hunting field) I do not admit as possible, if the lady has men about her who know their business in the horse way. If she has not such people about her, she is better without spurs decidedly; and there is another thing she is better without, namely, a horse of any sort.

If a horse is properly broken, and has a man about him who will give him plenty of work, and keep him from getting above himself, and his fair owner has been as well taught as her horse, she ought to be as safe on his back as in her brougham, in any kind of riding, except in exceptional cases in the hunting field. By exceptional cases I mean where a lady, unaccompanied by a good pilot, takes a line of her own when hounds are going fast in a big grass country, and rides (jealous of the field) at impracticable places. In such case she is likely enough to get down, horse and all. But even so—and I have witnessed more than one such accident—I have never found that the lady got hurt by the spur when she wore the sort I allude to; and again, I think it is only just to that clever loriner, Mr. Latchford, to say that he has invented a lady's stirrup which renders danger from it in the event of a fall next to impossible—certainly she cannot be dragged by it. In this stirrup there is no opening at the side by means of springs or complicated machinery of any sort. It requires neither diagram or drawing to describe it, because it is the perfection of mechanism—extreme simplicity. One has only to imagine an ordinary stirrup, rather elongated than usual from the opening for the leather, the bottom bar broad and flat; the latter perforated with two holes. Within the above-named stirrup another, a size smaller, but fitting nicely into it. On the lower side of the bottom bar of the inner stirrup two projections, or obtuse points of steel, which fit into the holes of the lower bar of the outer stirrup. Now, as long as the lady is in her saddle the inner stirrup must, from its mechanism, remain in its place; but in the event of her being thrown her weight acts upon the lower part of the outer stirrup, which turns over and releases the inner stirrup entirely.

To return, however, to the question proper of spurs for a lady, I must say that they are of the greatest assistance to her when, having acquired the necessary degree of steadiness on her horse, she desires to "wake him up." Too much whip is a bad thing. In riding in the country a lady must perforce have to open a bridle gate sometimes for herself, and if she is always using a whip to liven her her horse up, she will find it difficult to get him to stand still, even while she opens the lightest of gates. As regards the pupil in the school, I repeat she should be habituated to wear a spur as soon as her progress justifies it.

CHAPTER X.

THE CANTERING LESSON (*continued*).

HAVING satisfied himself as to the proficiency of his pupil in cantering "going large"—that is, round the school or *ménage*—the attention of the instructor should next be directed to teaching her to make the turns and circles, and execute the "half passage" with precision.

The use of these exercises is to confirm (while riding upon both snaffle and curb reins) the steadiness of hand and seat and true balance of the rider, because, although these may appear good enough while a lady is riding her horse on a straight line, or only with the turns at the corners of the school, many shortcomings will be detected when she attempts to turn him square from the boards, or asks him to make a true circle, in which the hind legs follow exactly over the same track as the fore legs.

To commence this lesson in proper form, the pupil should collect her horse, by reining him quietly back, then move him forward well up to the hand, at a walk and at a smart active pace. When she arrives at the centre marker at the end of the school, the master should give the word "down the centre," when the rider should turn her horse square to the right (assuming, as is usually the case, that she commences her lesson to that hand). The aids for turning at a walk having been already given, it is only necessary to say that the turn down the centre requires only a trifle stronger application of the left leg, to counteract any tendency of the horse to throw his haunches outwards, and that, looking steadily to the centre marker at the other end of the school, the pupil should sight that marker well between her horse's ears, and ride true and straight to it, taking care, by closing the leg in time, that the horse does not cut off any of the ground, but plants his near fore foot close to the boards and makes the corner equally square, because whenever a horse is allowed to "cut the corners off" he endeavours to get behind the bridle, and generally succeeds. The pupil, therefore, should be cautioned in time by the instructor, and if she fails to make good every inch of ground, the word "halt" should be given and the horse reined back. Arrived about midway down the school, the turns to the right should be made square from the boards, the horse's haunches kept under him so that he does not hit the side of the school with his hind feet. His doing which is at once a proof that he is out of hand. Arrived at the centre of the school, the words "right turn" should be given again, instead of allowing the pupil to ride right across the school to the boards on the opposite side. She should then ride a couple of lengths down the centre, and again turn her horse, by word from the master, square to the right, and once more to the left, when arrived at the boards. This, repeated two or three times, is a good preparation for executing the circle; in order to facilitate the correct riding of which, the master should cause his pupil to halt her horse at the side, and himself walk over the ground he desires her to ride over. If he does this correctly, the pupil will find little difficulty in riding the circle with precision.

Starting from a point close to the boards, a couple of horses' lengths in front of the pupil, the master should make an incline to the right, at an angle of about forty-five, until he is half-way between the boards and the centre of the school; he should then bring up his left shoulder, and make another incline at the same angle to the centre of the school. Down the centre he should walk straight, the distance of a horse's length; again bring up his left shoulder, and make two inclines to the side. The figure he will thus describe does not quite represent a circle as he walks; but when the horse is called upon to move his fore and hind legs on the same track, it will be a circle in his case as nearly as possible. Having caused the pupil to move her horse forward, the instructor should give her the aids for circling, which are a double feeling of the inward rein, the horse well supported with the outward, and well kept up to the hand by the leg.

In circling to the right, the horse to be well bent to the right, so that the rider can see his inward eye; fore and hind legs moving exactly on the same track, the horse not throwing his haunches out. The great use of this circling is, that as the horse changes his direction no less than six times in a small space, to keep him up to his work the lady must bring up her left shoulder as many times as the horse alters his direction. To do this, she must be quite supple in the waist, and circling is therefore a capital practice to insure this freedom of action at that portion of the figure. To render the lesson still more easy to the pupil, I have found it answer well, after walking over the ground, to mark it out on the tan with a stick. In military schools the circle to the right or left is followed by the "circle and change," in which, when arrived at the boards, the pupil, instead of turning the horse's head to the hand he is working to, changes the bend, and turns to the reverse hand. This, however, cannot be executed at a canter with due precision without the use of the right leg, and is therefore (in my opinion) better omitted in a lady's course of equitation, an additional reason being that, when she is taught to make the change at a canter, she can do it much more effectually and elegantly by the "half passage."

The circles having been neatly done, the pupil should rein her horse back, put him well upon his haunches, and strike him off at a collected canter, about five miles an hour, the cadence true, the position of the rider correct.

It is at this point that the instructor should begin carefully to get his pupil to supple herself in the saddle, while she still rides her horse well up to his work. It should be borne in mind that a horse cannot make turns or circles at the "pace of manœuvre" without considerable danger to himself and his rider, because at such a pace it is next to impossible to keep him fairly balanced, and he is liable, even on well-kept tan, to slip up, whereas at a very collected pace, with his haunches well under him, there is no danger whatever, although at first it will call very much upon the energy and close attention of the rider. Having her horse well into his bridle, the give-and-take action of the hand should now come gradually from the shoulder joint, and the pupil should be frequently reminded to avoid resisting the action of the horse in his canter, but to endeavour, on the other hand, to accompany him in his short stride. This is to be done by simply keeping both heels well down, the hands back, the waist bent slightly forward and perfectly supple, and avoiding too strong a grasp with the right leg upon the upper crutches of the saddle. The figure from the waist upwards, however, should be perfectly erect, leaning neither backwards nor forwards, either position being both unsafe and ungainly.

Nothing is more common than to see a lady sitting with the upper part of her figure bent forward in a canter, and, if not overdone, the effect is by no means ungraceful to the eye of a looker-on. But it is a habit likely to increase in degree, and unsafe in any case, because it is opposed to the principle of true balance.

With the shoulders well back, the body, neck, and head upright, the waist slightly bent forward, the hands well back, and acting by an easy play of the upper arm at the shoulder joint—sitting, in fact, with freedom in the saddle—the action of the horse at a collected pace will give the rider a slightly *gliding* motion from the cantle towards the pummels, and gradually she will thus acquire the habit of suppling herself on her horse; ready, however, at any moment "to seize her seat" (to use the expression of old Sam Chifney) by muscular grip if the horse flirts or plunges, which, however, it is difficult for him to do when going well within himself and up to his bridle.

The left leg at a canter should not be drawn back, as in trotting, but kept close to the horse's side, with the heel down, and the foot as nearly as possible under the knee. Of course, the above-described easy deportment in the saddle is not to be acquired in a single lesson; it requires considerable practice and close watching by both master and pupil. Once learnt, however, the lady has gained another important step in her equitation.

The length of time requisite to insure complete *souplesse* at this point is dependent upon several circumstances, over which the master has only a moderate amount of control.

The figure of the pupil is an important point in the matter. If she is naturally lithe and has been well suppled on foot, the task will be considerably easier. If, on the contrary, she is of a square figure—short in the neck and waist, and stiff in the shoulders—considerably more time is requisite. But with care, attention, and perseverance it can be acquired by all in early youth.

I know a lady who rides with both dash and judgment with hounds who is anything but a good figure; but she began under proper tuition when she was very young, and, although no longer so, she has preserved the *souplesse* and true balance acquired in her early days. Natural aptitude, too, is of great assistance to both master and pupil, and should be energetically developed by the former; at the same time, care should be taken that the pupil does not overrun her lessons.

As an instance of what can be accomplished even at a first essay by a lady gifted with natural talent for riding, I cannot refrain from relating the following:—Some years ago I chanced to be at the school of a fashionable riding master in London, when a class of young ladies was going through a ride. In the gallery from which I was observing them was also the mother of one of the young ladies who was riding, and of another much younger, who was standing by her side watching with the most intense interest the riding below. The younger lady was not more than ten or eleven years old, but of a form and figure exactly fitted for performing well in the saddle, being tall of her age, and lithe and supple in her movements. She did not speak, but I could see from the excitement of her manner, the glitter of her large dark eyes, and her changing colour, that she was heart and soul with the fair equestrians. The ride finished with a leaping lesson, and there was some capital jumping over a gorsed bar, hurdles double and single, and an artificial brook. The last performance completely overcame the little spectator in the gallery. Bursting into a violent fit of sobbing and weeping, she clutched her mother's dress, and cried convulsively, "Dear mamma, let me ride, let me ride." The lady, quite surprised and very much affected by the emotion and excited state of the child, nevertheless, refused, declaring she was too young. But the young supplicant for equestrian honours was not to be denied; she continued to implore and weep, and, the riding master coming to her aid, the mother gave way. Her little daughter was put on a quiet horse, and the master himself led him round the school at a walk, but this by no means satisfied our ambitious little tyro. "Let me trot," she said; "I am sure I can trot." The professor was quite sure she could not, and told her so; and, to convince her, he started the horse trotting, and ran by his side. He was never more mistaken. The lessons the pupil had been witnessing from the gallery must have made a strong impression on her mind; for, to the surprise of all of us, she caught the action of the horse at the first step, and made the best attempt at trotting I ever saw for a beginner. Feeling that trotting fatigued her, she asked to be allowed to canter, and this she did in very good form. But the crowning part of the thing was, that when we were about to take her off her horse, she begged to be allowed to have a jump. I confess, I thought the riding master wrong in consenting to this. But again our little friend electrified us all. A hurdle was put up, well sloped, so as to make the jump a very moderate one, the little pupil's hands placed, and her position rectified. No sooner had the horse turned the corner of the school, and before the riding master had time to check her, than the girl's eye lit up just as I had seen it in the gallery. She caught the horse fast by the head, hit him with her heel, put down her hands, and sat as though she had been hunting for years. It was too late to stop her, and any interference at the moment would have done more harm than good. With my heart in my mouth, I saw the horse go at the hurdle. He was one that had "an eye in every toe," and did not know how to make a mistake. But his daring little rider had roused him thoroughly, and he jumped high enough to clear a big fence, and far enough to take him over a small brook. Just as the horse took off, I shouted involuntarily, "Sit back;" and the little enthusiast answered as though my voice had been inspiration. Her lithe little figure was bent from the waist, precisely at the right moment; and she landed safe, except that the concussion threw her slightly up in the saddle. Her marvellous aptitude (talent the professionals would have called it) induced the riding master to let her make another attempt, and this time, putting her horse at the hurdle at the same dashing pace (which, by the way, with her wonderful nerve and confidence, made it easier for her), she sat in the saddle, as the old groom who tended the hurdles said, "as if she had grown there," and landed fair and true without jolt or concussion.

This young lady is now one of the most brilliant horsewomen in England. Her genius (if I may be permitted the expression), joined to close application and the best of opportunities of riding good horses, enabled her in a brief space to far outstrip all her youthful competitors, and in less than twelve months after the time I speak of she could execute most of the "bending lesson," at a canter as well as a professional rider, while over the country with hounds she was always close to her pilot, than whom there was no better man. This when she was barely thirteen years old.

Such instances of extraordinary aptitude, nerve and courage, combined with the necessary elasticity and physical power to ride, are very rare indeed; in fact, in a long experience of such matters, I do not know of a parallel case. Nevertheless, if the natural dash and fitness for riding possessed by this young lady had not been carefully watched, moulded into proper form, and restrained within due bounds, they would inevitably have run riot with her, and brought her to grief. It is in such cases as the above, or rather such as tend in that direction, that the tact and judgment of a riding master is required. If the young lady I speak of had been allowed, and the opportunity had offered, she would have mounted without hesitation any brute that would carry a saddle, and mischief, of course, would have resulted.

To return to the cantering lesson proper. When the instructor has succeeded in completely regulating the cadence of the horse in his pace and the position of his pupil, he should give her due caution to wait for the *last sound* of his word, to keep her body back and her leg close, supporting the horse well with the outward rein, and he should then give the word, well drawn out, gently and without hurry, "right turn," when the pupil should turn her horse from the boards with the same aids as at a walk, but more firmly applied, and if the horse leans upon her hand she should keep him up with her spur.

"Many a horse" (says the "Aid Book") "keeps a tolerable canter on a straight line, but when turned he feels too much constraint laid upon him, and leans upon the rider's hand. If at such a moment the rider yields the reins instead of closing the hand firmly on them, turning the little fingers up towards the waist, and closing the leg firmly, the horse comes upon his forehand."

Concise as the above passage is, it describes exactly what occurs on first making a turn at a canter, and it calls upon all the energy and attention of the pupil to keep the horse up to his work. But as in other exercises in the course of equitation, her reward will be in her thorough command over her horse under all circumstances, because by learning to ride him with such minute precision she is always able to anticipate his every movement.

The first three or four turns at a canter should be made square across the school, from side to side, and no second word should be given on arriving at the boards; the pupil turning her horse again to the right without any caution, and continuing to "go large" round the school until she again gets the word to turn. This practice will teach her to be constantly on the alert, and to maintain such a balance as will enable her in turning to move exactly on the same line as her horse, bringing her left shoulder up precisely at the right moment.

Three or four turns are quite sufficient for the first lesson, because the horse before completing these must go several times round the school, and the pupil should ride him well up to his bit. After a few turns, smoothly and correctly made, the pupil should bring her horse to the walk, halt, make much of him, and sit at ease.

Making much of a horse when he has performed well is always a judicious mode of letting him know that he has been doing right; at the same it affords him an interval of rest, which is quite necessary. This may appear absurd to those who are accustomed to see horses continue galloping for hours. But it must be remembered that the sort of work I have been endeavouring to describe is altogether artificial; that the animal thrown upon his haunches only goes through the lesson with considerable exertion, and that if he is kept too long at it, this can only be done by an amount of fatigue on the part of the rider which would be far from beneficial to a lady. The object of the lesson is to induct the pupil into a mode in which she can obtain complete mastery over her horse. It is, as it were, a gymnastic exercise for both steed and rider, and must not be persevered with too long at one time. After about ten minutes' rest the pupil should again collect her horse, rein him back, and prepare him again for cantering. She should then strike him quietly off, and ride him very collectedly, so as to be ready to make the circles. These should be made from about midway down the boards; and on the last sound of the words "circle right," the pupil should turn her horse's head from the boards, and, supporting him well with the left leg and rein, ride in a figure exactly similar to that she described at a walk. She will find, however, that the horse requires considerably more support in making the circles than he did in the simple turns. Being on the bend from the time he leaves the boards until he arrives at them again, the nicest riding is necessary to keep his fore and hind feet on the same track, and prevent him from throwing his haunches out. The pace, too, should be more collected than when the turns were made. Four miles to four miles and a half an hour is quite fast enough, and, if necessary, the horse must be halted and reined back several times in order to get him thoroughly collected. Two circles well done are quite sufficient. The pupil should then again halt, "sit at ease," and make much of her horse. By this time both he and the pupil will have gone through a tolerably severe lesson, because the collected pace necessary to execute it, and especially the circles, necessitates a great deal of cantering before a beginner can ascertain the true cadence—without which, and a considerable amount of support from her hand and leg, it is unsafe and useless for her to attempt her turns and circles; frequently, too, a horse will have to go several times round the school before the instructor can see the opportunity to give the word. Reining back again, and collecting him, call very much upon the horse's powers, while, on the other hand, over-fatigue is specially to be avoided as regards the pupil. After resting ten minutes or so, the lady should conclude this lesson by walking him quietly about till he is quite cool.

CHAPTER XI.

THE CANTERING LESSON (*continued*)—THE HALF PASSAGE AND CHANGE.

ALTHOUGH the last-named exercises belong, strictly speaking, more to the curriculum of the military riding school than to female equitation, still, to be able to execute them with precision is of great advantage to a lady, because they teach her that by getting a good bend on her horse, and placing him in a certain position by the application of the proper aids, she can compel him at her pleasure to canter with either near or off foot leading; and, although it may not be agreeable to her to keep her horse going with the near leg, unless she is riding on the off side, nevertheless, the practice of the half passage and change is an admirable, and indeed very elegant, mode of acquiring ready facility in the effective use of hand and leg. I have said before that the horse in the "half passage" places one foot before the other, instead of crossing his legs completely, as in the full passage. The former mode of progression enables the horse therefore to gain ground diagonally to his front, instead of moving upon a line at right angles with the boards as in the latter.

The aids by which the half passage is executed are the same as those of the "full passage," with the following exceptions. First, there is a lighter pressure of the leg on the outward side; and in the case of a lady it is necessary that she should use her whip on the off side behind the saddle alternately with her leg on the near side, in order to cause the horse to gain ground to the front, as well as to place one foot before the other.

After starting her horse at a walk, "going large," the rider should rein him back, collect and balance him—riding equally upon snaffle and curb reins—she should make the corner perfectly square; and when midway between it and the centre marker, the instructor should give the word "right half passage," upon which the pupil should still further collect her horse into the slow pace she used in the bending lesson, and, having arrived at the centre marker, she should bring the horse's forehand in, by a double feeling of the right rein; the outward leg closed, to prevent the haunches from flying out. The inward rein leads; the outward balances and assists the power of the inward. A pressure of the left leg causes the horse to place one foot before the other (see Aid Book). The whip used in alternate action with the leg will cause him to move to his right front, towards the boards.

A very light and delicate application of the leg, in unison with a similar application of the whip, is sufficient with a well-broken horse to enable the rider to do the "half passage" correctly at a walk. The point at which, strictly speaking, she should arrive at the boards is just midway between the ends of the school; and in a properly-regulated one there should always be a white marker on the wall, just above the place where the sockets for the leaping bar are inserted in it.

Keeping her eye upon this marker, the rider should lead her horse's forehand lightly with the right rein, maintaining an easy, playful, feeling of the snaffle in his mouth, and carefully balancing his every step with the left rein, while she presses him up to his work with the leg and whip. The horse's head should be bent to the right, so that his right eye is visible to the rider as she sits perfectly square in the saddle. The pace can scarcely be too slow, but every step must be taken up to the bridle, the horse's forehand up, and his haunches well under him.

In no part of a lady's course of equitation is it necessary for the instructor to pay more close attention to his pupil than in this: the temptation to the latter to relax her position, and sit, as it were, "all over the saddle" is great, from the difficulty she at first experiences in applying the aids effectually, and her anxiety to do well, causing her to twist her figure in pressing the horse with the left leg. The horse, too, is moving with his fore and hind feet in two distinctly different lines, which renders it far from easy, without considerable practice, to sit fair and square in the saddle. Close attention and quiet correction, however, will obviate all this.

Many people, I am aware, assert that riding with such precision is unnecessary to a lady. From this opinion I beg leave to dissent *in toto*, my idea being that a course of equitation for a lady means teaching her everything (less the lessons of the "Haute Ecole") connected with the subject, and that whether she chooses hereafter to practise the "bending lesson," "half passage," and change at a canter or not, a thorough knowledge of them will give her a facility of riding unattainable by any other means, and make her also thoroughly *au fait* to the reason for everything she does in order to control the animal under her.

Again, I can see no possible reason why the nicest precision should be considered unnecessary in a lady's riding any more than it is in music; and, to try back on my old simile, I submit that as the same scale is written for a Thalberg as for the fair daughter of the house who performs on the pianoforte for the *post prandial* amusement of paterfamilias, and inasmuch as the mode in which the music is performed is dependent in a great measure upon precision and practice, so in riding it is necessary to make a young lady acquainted with the principles of equitation in their minutest details, and carefully to watch that she executes them with the most rigid exactness.

To return to the half passage. On arriving at the boards the lady should halt her horse for a moment and make much of him, then rein him back, and again walk him round the school to the left. The half passage should then be done to that hand, reversing the aids, and using the whip instead of the left leg. This will bring the horse again upon the right rein. He should now be well put up to his work, and pressed smartly off at a very collected canter. The instructor should be most careful that the proper cadence in pace is arrived at before he gives the word, and should caution the pupil also that when she arrives at the boards she should bring her horse to the walk.

To facilitate this exercise also, it may be advisable in some cases to take the whole school instead of half of it; but in that case the horse should go over the same ground in the "half passage" at a walk, as he afterwards does at a canter.

When the exercise is done at the latter pace, no attempt should be made at the first effort to change the horse at the boards. The master should give the word very quietly directly the pupil turns the corner of the school, and she should then press her horse well up, and turn his head smoothly from the centre marker, applying her aids with firmness and decision, endeavouring at the same time to prevent him from hurrying his pace. This, however, at the first attempt, it is scarcely to be expected that she will accomplish.

If the whole school is taken, the point of arrival at the boards should be about a horse's length from the end, where he should be brought quietly to a walk, the rider for this purpose keeping the body back, turning the little fingers of both hands up towards the waist, and drawing the hands themselves well towards her waist. The bend of the horse's head should then be changed to the left, by allowing the off side reins to slip through the right hand about two inches, and drawing the near-side reins through the left hand, with the right, to an equal extent. The near-side reins should then be passed into the right hand, while with the left the rider "makes much" of her horse on the near side. This, of course, should only be done if he has executed the movement with reasonable precision, for (to repeat) perfection cannot be expected in the pupil's first effort.

Plenty of time should be taken between these "half-passage" lessons, because they are severe, calling very much upon the physical powers of both horse and rider.

In order to give both a fair chance, the lesson should be again done at a walk, then at a canter, the pupil carefully instructed on arriving at the boards to strike the horse off collectedly *to the left*. To do this she should quietly change the bend to that hand, carry her left foot well forward towards the horse's shoulder, so as to use an action of her leg reverse to that she had recourse to in striking him off to the right. She should keep him well bent, but well supported with the outward rein. When she has him in the corner of the school, and bent both in his neck and ribs (which in turning and putting his off fore foot into the angle must be the case, if she applies her whip smartly behind the flap of the saddle, and presses her left foot to his near elbow, keeping his forehand well up at the same time), he can scarcely refuse to strike off with his near leg; but it must be borne in mind that a lady cannot be expected to execute this movement with any certainty unless the horse has been previously taught by a man to obey the aids the lady applies as above directed. This, however, every breaker who knows his business can easily do.

When a fair amount of proficiency is acquired in this lesson, the change may be made from what is technically called a "half halt," which means simply that, the horse being thrown more upon his haunches, the aids are applied with great firmness, and the horse compelled to change his leg without being brought completely to the walk. The degree of proficiency, however, should be when the pupil can change her horse with certainty after halting him.

The pace at which the half passage is done should be very collected, and, I repeat, if the rider and horse do it only reasonably well (that is, the latter continuing true and united in his pace, and changing freely after being halted), that for some little time it should be considered sufficient, and every allowance made for the fact that the lady, unlike the male rider, cannot give support to her horse with both legs.

Most likely at first the horse will throw his haunches out a little, and the rider slightly lose her position. Practice and the close application most ladies give to riding will suffice to correct all this, and in due time the pupil will be able to execute the lesson with smoothness and ease to herself and her horse. She will then be sufficiently advanced to commence cantering on the curb rein alone. This, as regards finish in the rider's hand, is in equitation what tone is in music. Every motion of the little finger, or the slightest turn of the wrist, acts upon the curb when it is unrelieved by the snaffle with so much more power, that the greatest care is necessary to keep the bridle hand steady at first, and to avoid anything approaching to suddenness or roughness of action.

This steadiness is best accomplished by causing the pupil to ride with the reins arranged military fashion, with the snaffle reins hanging over the full of the left hand, the off side rein uppermost, and the right hand holding the end of the curb reins, as before described, which affords greater facility for easing and feeling them than can at first be expected, when the action is given altogether from the left wrist. In the latter case, the hand without considerable practice would be far too heavy, even when the arm was kept quite firm, and unbearably heavy to the horse if there was any motion from the shoulder of the rider.

I must repeat that the lines of action of the little finger of the bridle hand are four—namely, towards the right and left shoulder respectively, according as the rider desires to turn the horse right or left; and towards his neck and her own waist, as she wishes to collect, rein back, or move him forward.

Now, while in trotting on the curb rein only the hand and arm should be kept as steady as possible, in order that the horse may make a free *appui* between mouth and hand, "taking hold a little of the latter;" in cantering the direct reverse of this is the case, and the hand of the rider should give and take to every stride of the horse.

It is in the mode of timing these give-and-take motions in exact harmony with the action of the horse that fine and finished hands consist; and I will endeavour to give an idea of the readiest way in which this delicate manipulation may be acquired, with as much precision as the fair rider can exercise when pressing the keys of a pianoforte.

Let us suppose, then, that in preparing for the cantering lesson on the curb, in order nicely to collect the horse, the reins are drawn quietly through the left hand by the right, as above described, the object being to rein the horse back a step or two, and balance him well with forehand up and haunches under him. By the above-named drawing up of the reins a firmer *appui* is created against the horse's mouth. By closing both leg and whip, however, while still maintaining this *appui*, the horse will step back. The instant he does the reins should be yielded to him, and he will bend in the poll of the neck and yield to his rider's hand. So that the *appui* is then scarcely perceptible. This alternate action of hand and leg, aided by the whip, should be repeated just as many times as it is desired to rein the horse so many steps backward, the latter moving very slowly; a couple or three steps for the purpose above named are always sufficient. To move the horse to the front again at a walk, the leg should be closed, and the reins eased until he moves forward, when he should be again collected. But if the rider desires to strike him off at once at a canter, at the moment she eases her hand she should apply her spur smartly just behind the girth, and touch the horse lightly on the off shoulder with her whip. Being properly bent and prepared, he will then strike off with his right leg first, and well within himself; but having eased the reins as the horse takes his first short stride forward, the rider should feel them again the next instant, keeping her left hand well back, her arm steady, and manipulating the reins with the right hand and the fingers of the left, so that she feels them just as the horse's fore foot is on the ground, and eases them as he raises it.

This may appear to the uninitiated a very difficult matter, but in reality it is not at all so, any more than it is difficult in dancing to keep time to music, or for the musician to count the time to himself; and by careful watching it can be mastered as well as either of the above, or the stroke in swimming.

Anybody who has witnessed a cavalry field day will have noticed that the regimental band and the action of the horses both in trotting and cantering past the commanding officer are in exact harmony; and many people believe that the horses are taught to canter to the music. The reverse of this, however, is the case. The leader of the band, having himself passed through a course of equitation, knows the exact cadence of the pace of manœuvre, and regulates the time of the music accordingly; but it is because he is able to count the time of the horses' footfall so well that he is also able to set the time of the music. In like manner the fair equestrian, with a little practice, can learn to count the time of her horse's canter to herself, and regulate the action of her hand accordingly.

The pupil must throw plenty of *life* into her riding, and, while she sits easily and flexibly as regards her whole figure on the saddle, should keep the horse equally upon his mettle. In a riding school he requires more calling upon than when out of doors, and more "pressing up," as it is technically called; but when once the rider has him going, well balanced, and bending nicely, the great thing is to "let well alone," and not ask too much, by which she would only fret and upset him. In bringing the horse to the walk, the pupil should be cautioned to feel him up very gradually, avoiding any sudden jerk on his mouth. The gradual stronger feeling for two or three strides, of the taking action of the hand, followed by a much slighter giving of the reins, will bring the horse smoothly to the walk. The body of the rider should be inclined slightly back from the perpendicular.

When the lady has acquired ease and freedom in riding on the curb, the turn, circles, "half passage" and change may be practised, close attention being given that the aids are applied smoothly and quietly.

After a few such lessons, the pupil may commence riding with the left hand entirely unassisted by the right. For this purpose it is necessary first to carry that portion of the reins held in the right hand over the middle joint of the fore finger of the left; close the thumb firmly down on them, and drop the slack of the rein to the off side of the saddle near the horse's shoulder.

The give-and-take action must at first be from the wrist only, the arm being kept firm, and the hand opposite the centre of the body.

For a time this will be a little difficult, especially in turning, when the rider has only the motion of the little finger to depend upon for the action of the bit in the horse's mouth; but by supporting the horse well with the leg and whip, she will find that he will presently answer readily to her aids. In turning to the right, the hand must be turned with the knuckles up, and the little finger down towards the left shoulder, the whip pressed to the horse's side, and the leg kept close, in order to make the turn square. In turning to the left, the little finger should be directed inwards and upwards towards the right shoulder, and the left leg pressed to assist the turn, while the whip on the off side insures its squareness. The wrist must be quite easy and supple. In collecting, reigning back, halting, or bringing the horse to the walk, the action by which he is restrained should again at first be altogether from the wrist, because motion from the shoulder would be too heavy. In yielding to the horse, nothing more is necessary than to turn the knuckles up and the little finger towards the horse's neck.

By degrees, as the pupil learns to command her horse riding in this form she must be instructed once more to give free and mobile action to the arm at the shoulder joint, as when riding on both snaffle and curb reins. But at first firmness of the arm is essential to give steadiness to the hand. A good deal has been said about turning horses by pressure of the rein against the neck without acting upon the metal in his mouth; and opinions very diverse have been expressed on this point. With all deference to the disputants, I submit that both are right and both wrong in some respects. For instance, when the rider has the reins divided and the hands well apart (a section of the lady equitation I propose to say something about hereafter), if the rider turns the horse square to the right or left he must use his legs as well as his hands, and imperceptibly perhaps to himself (even if he has not been taught by rule) he closes both the outward leg and feels the outward rein firmly, in order to support the horse and prevent him from falling, which otherwise he would be in danger of doing. Now, this support with the outward rein causes it to press against the horse's neck, and to some extent gives him the indication of the rider's will. But still it is simply impossible to do this without acting on the snaffle or bit rein, as the case may be, on one side or the other, as long as the reins are attached to a bit of any sort. And after all, it is the leg which gives the surest indication of the rider's will.

One sees a lad in an Irish fair riding with a flat-headed halter turned through the horse's mouth, and, with the rope only on one side, he will put the horse through his paces, jump him, and turn him to either hand. There is no metal at all in the mouth, although the hemp is not a bad substitute; but the rope being only on one side, it is evident that it is not pressure upon the neck that turns the horse, but the action of the boy's leg against the intercostal muscles of the horse, and the inflection of the lad's body to the hand he desires to turn to.

Moreover, in the case, let us say of a dragoon, we will suppose at riding school drill, it would be utterly out of the question to turn horses by pressure on the neck and preserve order at the same time. Let us suppose a double ride—seven mounted men on either side of a school or *manége*. They are going large round the place, and the instructor gives the word "Right and left turn." If each man of the fourteen were to turn his horse by pressure of the reins against the neck, instead of by the aid of leg and hand, the result would be that in place of making a square turn at right angles with the boards, each horse would describe a segment of a circle, more or less large, according to the susceptibility of his neck, and the stiffness or otherwise of his ribs. The consequence would be that the two sides, instead of passing left hand to left hand through the intervals (and it must be remembered that there is little room to spare), would be on the top of each other, and in confusion at once. And if this would be bad at a walk, it would be still worse at a canter. In either case it would be impossible, by the application of such aids, to preserve the dressing. The above, I submit, is a sufficient reason, where the utmost precision in riding is required, why turning a horse by the action of the rein against his neck (if, indeed, it can be done at all without the leg) is objectionable; and another objection in the case both of the dragoon and the lady rider is that the motions by which such aids could be applied are *too wide* for neat and elegant riding.

Horses in their breaking may be taught to answer all sorts of "cross aids;" but for simplicity and ease of comprehension there is nothing in equitation so good as the system practised in the German and our own cavalry riding schools, the proof of which lies in the fact that, although years ago one did not get even an average amount of intelligence as a rule in our rank and file, yet every cavalry soldier could readily understand the simple system upon which he was taught. It is because that system forms, after all, the basis of much that applies to female equitation that I have so frequently quoted from and alluded to it.

When the instructor finds that his pupil is quite at her ease, riding her horse with one hand only, that she can do this, giving due freedom of action to the arm at the shoulder joint, has perfect command of him, and plenty of liberty and confidence in her own deportment on his back, he should take her out and ride with her in the park or road, and subsequently prepare her to extend her horse at a gallop, and commence her leaping lessons.

At this stage a more finished style of equestrian toilette will of course be adopted, in lieu of the loose habiliments hitherto used.

I do not pretend to lay down any arbitrary rule on this subject. Much of course depends upon the taste of the lady herself, and in this respect English ladies are pre-eminent; a good deal also upon the judgment and experience of those about her. But as I have good opportunies of seeing the best types of fashionable attire for ladies' riding, I venture to suggest some of them.

CHAPTER XII.

Dress for Park Riding, and the Extended Paces.

In no department of the charming art of dressing well is a lady so much shackled by conventional usages as in her "get up" for riding. In all other kinds of dress, from the full Court costume to simple morning wrapper, such is the almost endless variety of style that there is something to suit every woman, from the lady of high degree to "Dolly Varden," and the "Molly Duster;" and the selection made is conclusive as to the good or bad taste of the wearer. In riding dress it is altogether different. "Chimney pot" hats, tight-fitting jackets, and flowing skirts of orthodox dark rifle-green seem to be *de rigueur*, whatever may be the figure, style, or complexion of the wearer. I submit (and in this opinion I am borne out by several accomplished lady riders, to one of whom I am indebted for the following suggestions) that this is wrong, and that some modifications as regards shape and colour would be advantageous both as regards the comfort of the ladies themselves, and as a matter of taste.

To begin with head-dress. It is manifest that whereas a lady of tall, lithe figure, with an oval Grecian style of face, and classical contour of head, will appear to the greatest advantage on horseback in a plain or gentleman's hat, and with her hair so arranged as to show the outline of the head and neck, one of the Hebe style of beauty, particularly if slightly inclined to the "*embon.*," if so accoutred, would not look by any means well. Yet one constantly sees the same sort of head-dress worn by ladies whose general style is in direct contrast, the reason presumably being that fashion admits of such little latitude for choice.

Again, as regards the jacket. A lady of slight figure (for effect) can scarcely wear anything that fits too close, consistently with her freedom of motion; but the fair equestrian whose proportions are not "sylph like" is badly equipped in such a garment.

To revert to the hat for the latter type of lady, the most becoming style seems to be one with a low crown, and brim more or less wide, according to the features of the wearer, as such hats admit of great variety, both in material, and, what is more important, in colour; and consequently it is not difficult for a lady to obtain that which is exactly suitable to her both as regards feature and complexion.

Some of these hats for park or road riding, ornamented with ostrich or other feathers, are exceedingly elegant and becoming, and protect the skin from the rays of the sun, without any necessity for a veil, which cannot be said of the plain black or gentleman's hat. For the hunting field, of course, feathers or ornaments are out of place; but nevertheless most elegant low-crowned, wide-rimmed hats, made of fine felt and without ornament, of shapes suitable to every class of feature, are obtainable in Melton, and I presume are equally accessible in London.

The form of jacket most suitable for a lady whose proportions incline to fulness is a tunic, made Hussar fashion, that is, it should have two seams in the back and be well sprung inwards towards the waist without fitting tight; the short skirt made full, and reaching well down to the saddle; the sleeves wide. Broad braiding judiciously arranged on such tunics, too, will have the effect of considerably diminishing the appearance of redundant fulness of figure in the wearer.

Two rows of braiding, commencing at the lower edge of the tunic behind, should bend inwards towards the waist; but instead of diverging thence to the shoulder points, as in a military coat, should pass over the shoulders, about midway between them and the neck, and thence be continued with a turn (ornamental or plain) to the front of the tunic on both sides, and reaching down to its lower extremity. There should be no braiding round the bottom edges of the jacket. These tunics can be made either single or double breasted, but in either case should have broad lappets in front;

and neckties of any colour suitable to the wearer's complexion, arranged as a gentleman ties his neckcloth, and fastened with gold horseshoe pins, jewelled or plain, are very effective. The single-breasted tunic should be fastened with hooks and eyes, covered by the braid; the double-breasted jacket should fasten with plain silk buttons. The advantage of these tunics is that, while they afford plenty of room to the rider, and while they in no way cramp her flexibility in the saddle, they tend to diminish to a degree scarcely conceivable the appearance of redundant fulness or squareness of form, and give a very elegant *tournure* to a figure that would look by no means well in a tight-fitting jacket.

Again, neckties of moderately large pattern, and ornaments in the way of feathers and pins, or other fastenings for the cravat, all tend to diminish to the eye the appearance of weight and size, and as a rule, are as becoming on horseback to ladies of full figure as rigid plainness in habits, collars, &c., are to those of spare and delicate form. It should be borne in mind that it is on the off side that the figure of a lady equestrian is most critically noticed by the observer. On the near side the skirt has a great effect in increasing or diminishing the apparent size and form of the rider. On the off side every defect in form or dress is patent, and it is on the off side that the gentleman attendant rides. Close-fitting jackets, then, I repeat; plain gentleman's hats, with or without lace lappets, and extreme simplicity of get up, will be most effective on the off side in the case of a lady of slight figure. The style of hat and tunic I have attempted to describe is most suitable to those whose *physique* is more developed.

As regards skirts, a fair amount of fullness, according to the size of the rider, for road or park, gives a very graceful appearance on the near side, care of course being taken that the habit is not so long as to admit of the horse treading on it. For hunting skirts can scarcely be too circumscribed, as long as they afford the wearer freedom of action.

A word now about colours. I repeat that except in the arbitrary dictum of fashion there is no warranty for the all but universal prevalence of dark rifle-green for riding habits. It must be evident that a lady who is a "brunette" will look far better in a riding dress the colour of which is dark chocolate or purple than she will in green of any sort; and on the other hand a "blonde" would be more suitably attired in a habit of a shade of light blue suitable to her complexion than in anything of more sombre hue. Again, in the hunting field why should our atrician ladies who grace these sporting réunions with their presence, and go as straight and well as any men, shewing always in the front rank, be debarred by fashion or conventional usage from wearing scarlet jackets. Scarlet is worn on foot—for opera cloaks, in shawls, in whole dresses. Why not scarlet on horseback? I saw a lady this season riding with one of our crack Midland packs who wore a scarlet jacket of very fine cloth; a light blue silk cravat, fastened with a diamond horseshoe pin; a skirt of very dark blue, and a plain man's hat of Melton style. She was a blonde with golden hair, mounted on a bright chestnut blood-like hunter; and, as she was of slight, lathy figure, and rode exceedingly well, the *ensemble* was quite charming. This lady was the cynosure of all eyes, not only on account of her capital riding but her dress, which I heard deprecated by some as "*too loud.*" My humble opinion was that it was exactly in harmony with the place and the sport, most becoming to the wearer, and calculated to give *dash* and *brilliancy* to the *coup d'œil* afforded by the field as they streamed away after the hounds; moreover, the lady herself had that thoroughbred stamp and aristocratic bearing that would have rendered any innovation in equestrian costume admissable in her case. But when the complexion and style of any lady admits of it, I can see no reason why she should not wear scarlet with foxhounds as well as her brother or her husband. In summer time, too, is not dark riflegreen or any dark colour and thick cloth which attracts the rays of the sun to the certain discomfort of the wearer an absurdity, when the fair equestrian would look far better, because more seasonably attired, in light grey, light blue, or even in a habit of perfectly white linen, or similar fabric?

As I have ventured to point out a pleasing alteration of conventional dress in the hunting field, I trust I may be pardoned for describing what appeared to me an equally consistent innovation in summer costume for the saddle. Last summer I saw four young ladies taking an early morning canter over a breezy down in this neighbourhood. The weather was sultry. Three of the ladies wore habits of different shades of grey, according to their respective complexions, the fabric evidently very thin. Their equipment was completed by felt hats of different shapes, exceedingly becoming. The fourth lady, who was very fair, wore a perfectly white habit, made, I presume, of linen; the jacket edged with a narrow light blue cord; her headdress was a yachting hat of Tuscan straw, encircled by and also fastened under her chin with light blue ribbon. In the front of her jacket she wore a moss rosebud. She was riding an Arab-like blood horse, and being, like her companions, not only well mounted, but a first-rate horsewoman, the effect was not only pleasing to the eye and full of "dash," but, I am sure, most conducive to the comfort of the fair riders themselves. Fashion apart, I may fairly ask, would not these four ladies have looked equally well, and felt as much at their ease, in Rotten Row as on the springy Leicestershire turf? I devoutly hope yet to see some of the leaders of fashion in the gay London season inaugurate some such change as I venture to suggest; and certain I am if they did so, Rotten Row in the month of May would present a brilliant Watteau-like appearance, very different from that produced by the prevalence of sombre colours now worn by the equestrian *habitués* of that fashionable ride.

To return to our fair pupil (having made such selection of riding dress as is most suitable to her style). Her first outdoor rides should be taken on some quiet and little frequented road until she becomes accustomed to control her horse; for there is a great difference in the form of going of the same animal in the riding school and on the road, as many horses that require considerable rousing in the school are all action and lightheartedness out of doors.

On the road, especially when they are hard, walking and trotting should be the pace, the pupil riding equally on snaffle and curb reins; the pace free and active; the trot about eight to eight and a half the hour.

Cantering should never be practised on hard ground, as it is certain, sooner or later, to cause mischief to the horse's legs. Where there is a good broad sward by the roadside, as in the Midland counties, a good stretching canter for miles may always be had where the ground is good going. But such places are not to be found in the neighbourhood of the metropolis; and it is necessary therefore to select some open common, such as Wimbledon or Wormwood Scrubs, for cantering at first.

By degrees the pupil should be accustomed to ride through thoroughfares where there is considerable traffic, and may then make her *début* in Rotten Row; and here I may remark that nobody, lady or gentleman, should ever attempt riding in this fashionable equestrian resort until they have thorough command of their horses, and, indeed, know scientifically what riding is. The place, strictly speaking, is a ride intended for royalty alone; and I believe I am correct in saying that the admission of the general public to it is by no means a matter of right. Great pains are bestowed to keep it in good order throughout the year; especially, it is always soft and good for a horse's legs. But as a great concourse of equestrians, male and female, is always in the Row in the London season, and as the horses are nearly all well bred and high couraged, there is considerable danger, both to themselves and others, in persons with indifferent seats and hands venturing to ride in the fashionable crowd, the danger being considerably enhanced by the fact that such people are altogether ignorant of the risk they are running. For my own part, after seeing some corpulent citizen rehearsing "John Gilpin" in Hyde Park, with his trousers half-way up to his knees, and his feet the wrong way in the stirrups, the wonder has always been to me not that accidents occur in Rotten Row, but that there are not a great many more.

There are adventurous ladies, too, who occasionally create a sensation among the crowd, not at all flattering to themselves if they only knew the sentiments of those about them; and I really think it would be a capital plan to appoint some competent gentle-

H

men to take charge by turns of the Row in the London season, and order the mounted police on duty quietly to see everybody out of it who was unable to command their horses. Matters, since the mounted constables have been put on, are not quite so bad as formerly; but there is plenty of room for improvement still, both as regards dogs, pretty horsebreakers, and tailors.

At all events, I recommend any man taking a young lady into the Park in the height of the London season " to have his eyes about him " in every direction, lest some "dashing equestrian," male or female, should come bucketing a horse in rear of his charge, and to keep a close watch also upon the latter—to see that she *rides her horse* all the time she is in the place, keeping him well into his bridle, which reduces to a minimum the chances of his suddenly flirting.

Elsewhere I have gone at considerable length into the subject of possible accidents in the Park. It is perhaps necessary that I repeat the gist of it here, which is simply that no young lady, however accomplished a horsewoman she may be, should be allowed by her friends to ride in the Row unattended by a male companion, who is not only a thoroughly good horseman, but accustomed to ride beside a lady and *anticipate* anything in the shape of bad manners on the part of her horse; that the attendance of a groom, who rides at a considerable distance in rear of the lady (whatever appearance of conventional style it may give to the fair equestrian), is utterly useless to her in case of accident, nay, in more than one instance that I have known has been productive of it from the groom galloping up at a critical moment, and still further exciting the lady's horse. Finally, that no lady should ever ride a horse of high breed and courage that has been allowed to " get above himself," by remaining day after day in the stable, or having insufficient work, when exercised, to keep down exuberant freshness.

There is no danger to a thoroughly good horsewoman in riding a horse that is "light-hearted." But there is risk to everybody, man or woman, in riding one " mad fresh," ready to jump out of his skin, as the grooms say, in a crowd of other horses.

For my own part, of two evils, I would rather see a lady jammed into a lane with twenty or thirty horses, after hounds had just got away, and everybody was struggling to get out, than I would see her in the Park unattended by a gentleman, and mounted upon a well-bred horse that was very fresh. I do not by any means deprecate riding in the Row. It is a splendid piece of riding ground, and relieved to some extent, as it now is, of overcrowding by the ride on the upper side of the Park ;' it is a glorious place for a canter. But I repeat, let everybody who takes a horse there be able to ride him, and have eyes for his neighbours as well as himself; and especially let gentlemen who attend ladies there be always on the *qui vive* for the adventurous Gilpins and "pretty horse-breakers."

The canter for the Row, conventionally and wisely, should be almost as collected as that of the riding school. It is an understood thing, in fact, that no lady or gentleman (properly so called) "sets a horse going" there; and trotting when practised should also be done very collectedly, both paces admitting of the display of talent and proficiency in equitation of the rider.

For the more extended paces, it is necessary again to have recourse to open heath or common ; and, before the pupil attempts to "set her horse going," the difference between cantering, in the "andante" pace, and galloping, should be clearly explained to her. The main difference in this cantering is to some extent an artificial pace, because, when practised collectedly, the greater weight of the horse is brought from his forehand on to his haunches; and the shorter the pace, the more his weight is on his hind legs. It is for this reason that very collected cantering should not be continued for any great length of time, from its tendency to strain the hocks, nevertheless cantering, like trotting, cannot fairly be pronounced altogether artificial, because anybody who has had the handling of a great number of young horses must have seen many of them running loose who would canter the length of a paddock at quite a short pace, both legs on the same side (generally the near side); and I have seen a foal at a mare's foot trot, true and fair, for a considerable distance.

Gallopping, however, like walking, is a perfectly natural pace, although it is a mistake to say that in the gallop the horse moves both fore and hind legs together, in what is frequently termed "a succession of jumps." That he does this in his top speed, and especially in making a supreme effort, as in a desperate finish of a race, is perfectly true: but it is equally certain that at half or three quarter speed he is leading with either near or off fore leg, and that anything but a *full speed* gallop is simply a very extended canter. Any man who has ridden a race must know that where the distance is great, say four miles or more, and men do not force the pace, for perhaps two-thirds of the way every horse (say of a score of them) will be leading with either near or off leg, generally the former, and that a very hot excitable horse, eager to get to the front, will *change his leg* when he finds his rider keeps his hands down, and his horse back. It may be said that this is not galloping but cantering; but I beg to assure all those who maintain this opinion that such a canter is faster than any gallop resorted to, apart from racing, that, in short, such a gallop is a very extended canter. Whatever the term, however, may be most applicable to it, half racing speed is quite as fast as a lady will have occasion to ride, unless in cases of desperate emergency. At such speed the horse has altogether a different balance to that maintained in the short canter; and, although he does not go altogether on his shoulders, still, to afford him freedom of action, he must be allowed to extend his head and neck, because, if too much bent, his action will be clambering, instead of sending him freely to his front.

To gallop a horse in good form the lady should adopt a different arrangement of the reins to any heretofore used. It is simply to divide them, so that the little fingers of both hands pass between the snaffle and curb reins, the latter under the little finger, and a little longer than the former, the *appui* being principally upon the snaffle, although there should be no slack rein on the curbs. Her hands should be kept well apart, and as low down as she can get them. The reason for separating the hands is, that it is far more difficult for a lady to set her hands down than for a man to do the same thing, because the front forks of the saddle are very much in her way.

If, however, she rides with a saddle, the off side crutch of which is "cut down," and she places her right hand outside her right knee, and her left hand outside the near side upper crutch, she will have the reins at nearly the same angle, and about the same feeling on the horse's mouth, as would be obtained by a man in setting his horse going.

In order to counteract any tendency of this position of the hands to interfere with the rider's proper balance, the left foot should be carried well forward, while the leg is pressed firmly against the third crutch, and an equally firm grasp of the upper crutch is taken with the right knee. A slight bend forward of the figure from the waist upwards is admissible, but great care should be taken by the instructor that this is not overdone, but regulated by the angle at which the left foot is placed. With the slight bend forward, however, there should be no rounding of the back or shoulders, or dropping of the head. Neither should the hands be allowed to get too forward; they will be somewhat in advance of their position at a canter, but not be more than six or eight inches from the body—the hands with the knuckles upwards, the elbows only slightly bent.

The ground selected for this exercise should be well known to the instructor—sound, good-going turf, perfectly free from rabbit holes or rotten places. The pace should be gradually increased from a free canter to about half-racing speed, the master making the pace himself, and carefully watching his pupil in every stride her horse takes. The lady should be instructed to let her horse "take fairly hold" of her, and press him with the leg until he strides freely along in his gallop. She should keep her hands shut firmly on the reins, and rest the former against the saddle. The horse then, while taking well hold of her, will not *pull*, nor will she pull an ounce against him, the consequence being that when she desires to decrease her speed, she has only to lean back gradually from her galloping position, bringing the body first perfectly upright, and then inclining back at about the same angle she previously carried it forward, raise her hands up from the saddle, and carry them back to her waist, while she turns the little fingers inwards and upwards towards it, which will cause her to feel the curb reins with a double feeling to the snaffle, and in about a dozen strides she can thus collect her horse into a steady canter and bring him subsequently to a walk. The length and speed of these rides must be carefully regulated by the master according to the nerve and strength of his pupil. Without a fair amount of both nerve and physical power such gallops should not be attempted at all. Where there is plenty of both, a half-mile spin is admissible to begin with, and, with good going ground, this may be increased gradually to a couple of miles. The instructor should be very careful in cautioning his pupil to diminish the speed of her horse by degrees and in the manner above described, especially avoiding any sudden pull at him, or any unsteadiness of the hands. Carefully practised, these gallops will give the pupil great freedom and confidence in the saddle; and they are, moreover, wonderful promoters of health.

CHAPTER XIII.

The Leaping Lesson.

I COME now to a section of our courses of instruction, which, if not as some suppose the most difficult to impart or acquire, is nevertheless of great importance. The principles, however, upon which a horse "does a fence" neatly and safely, and those upon which depend the secure riding of the lady, once properly understood, the rest is a question of practice, the thorough training of the horse and his complete fitness for his task being assumed. The two latter points are, however, of such vital consequence that I will endeavour to direct attention to several matters connected with them, which I trust may be useful.

In the first place, then, it should be borne in mind that whereas every horse of every breed in the world can be taught to jump, jumping comes so aptly to some as to be perfectly natural, and no more trouble to them with a fair weight than walking or galloping. Such horses are easily taught to be *clever;* that is to say, to do "doubles," "in and out," and crooked places, with almost the surefootedness of a goat, as well as to jump clean timber or fly sixteen or eighteen feet of water. The sort of animal I speak of is fond of jumping, and consequently when carefully broken learns to *balance himself* with the greatest nicety; and, provided the ground is sound, you cannot get him down, while he does not know what refusing means, except in the case of utterly impracticable places.

It is upon such horses, or those which approach the nearest to them in their qualifications, that a lady should be mounted, not only for the hunting field itself, but in her initiation in the riding school into the art of riding her horse over a fence. Horses that rush at their jump, are hot-headed, or intemperate in any way, are utterly unfit for a lady to attempt leaping with, either indoors or out. There should be blood and quality undoubtedly, as well as substance and power, but these must be joined to the best of temper. Possibly the very perfection of a horse exists in that wonderful little animal the Lamb, who has just exhibited at Liverpool the most extraordinary feats of *cleverness* and endurance, coupled with splendid action, speed, and temper, ever yet shown by any horse. The form in which, galloping at top speed, he jumped over two horses lying *hors de combat* right in his way, and cleared both and their riders without further injury to any, will live always in the memory of those who witnessed it; while his unflinching and determined effort to win under a weight that scarcely admitted of hope stamp the Lamb as a horse without equal in our day. In my opinion no price in reason could be too much to ask or give for such animal.

A short time ago I had the great honour and privilege accorded me by his noble owner of a close inspection at his private training quarters of this unrivalled little equine gem; and I am bound to say that, although I never quite believed in perfection of a horse until I saw the action, manner, and general form of the Lamb, as far as my judgment or experience goes, I freely accord to him the palm over every horse I have seen in a lifetime spent among horseflesh in one quarter or another of the world; but, although it is not possible in my humble opinion to find his equal as a cross-country horse, our endeavours should be directed to obtain for a lady hunter that which approximates most closely to the Lamb. Let me briefly point out what are the qualities that render such horses the fittest for carrying a lady to hounds.

In the first place, the connecting points of such an animal are so true in their relative adjustment, that while in galloping he does not *clamber* or fight the air, he goes with action so safe as always to clear any of those apparently insignificant obstacles, which too often bring to grief a gallant-looking steed and his fair rider. When "ridge and furrow" (as must sometimes occur) run the wrong way, he can go safe from land to land; and this is of greater consequence to a lady's riding than many suppose. The stamp of horse I speak of, too, will gallop with his hind legs well under him, while he maintains a proper balance of his fore hand without getting his head too low. He will do his fences without rush or passion, and measure his distance to perfection.

Secondly, his breeding gives him the power to endure through long runs, while his temper prevents that feverish excitement so detrimental in its reaction on a hot horse after a long day's hunting.

To return to the detail of the leaping lesson. This should always be commenced either in a riding school or in a space so inclosed as to do away as nearly as possible with any chance of the horse refusing. It is not possible always to procure one that is quite a "Lamb;" and, however well trained the animal on which the fair pupil is put, no possible temptation to do wrong should ever be allowed to remain in his way. A gorse-bound bar, a wattled hurdle or common sheep hurdle are all equally good for the first attempt, care being taken not to make the leap too high. But I do not, from experience, believe in putting the bar or other obstacle on the ground, because the effort a well-broken horse makes to clear it is so slight, that it puts the rider off her guard; and when afterwards he rises higher in his jump, he is very apt to shift her in the saddle. There is a very natural inclination on the part of a tyro in riding, lady or gentleman (having seen a horse jump under another person), to suppose that some effort of the hand is necessary *to lift* the horse over the obstacle.

It should be the duty of the instructor carefully to warn his pupil against any such effort, and in the first attempt to attend only to her true equilibrium, while she presses the horse well up to his bridle, keeping her hands perfectly steady, well back, and well down. She should take a firm hold of the upper crutch of the saddle with her right knee; sit well *into* the saddle, and not on the back of it, because the further back she sits, the greater the concussion when the horse alights. She should put her left foot well home in the stirrup, and press her leg firmly against the third crutch, while she keeps the left knee quite flexible, and the left foot well forward. She should draw her figure well up from the waist, which should be bent slightly forward; and she should avoid *stiffening* the waist, because it is from that point that she is able to throw the upper part of the figure backwards at the proper moment, and at the true angle, to preserve her balance. She should direct her glance straight between the horse's ears, and well in front of him to the end of the school, because if she looks down at her hands or the bar, she relaxes her upright position. The horse should be led up to the bar by the instructor, who should be able to jump lightly over the obstacle with the horse; and another assistant should follow with a whip, the presence of which the horse will recognise in an instant, without any noise being made with it, and he will go at once into his bridle, and "take hold" of the rider's hand. A groom should hold the end of the bar or hurdle so lightly, that if the horse touches it, it will fall; while another groom should stand in such a position, about a horse's length to half a one outside the instructor, as to do away with all chance of the horse swerving from any nervous action of the rider's hand.

In jumping, at first the pupil should ride entirely upon the snaffle rein. In fact, for early leaping lessons, it is best to put a good broad reined snaffle in the horse's mouth, instead of a double bridle, because it prevents any confusion about the reins, and consequent derangement of nerve in the pupil. On approaching the bar, the latter should incline the body back from the waist upwards, at such an angle, that a line from the back point of the shoulder would fall about a couple of inches behind the cantle of the saddle. This is not according to the strict formula laid down by high-class professors of equitation; on the contrary. "The Aid Book" tells us that "the body should be inclined forward as the horse rises, and backwards as he alights." But I have found in teaching *ladies* to jump their horses that, particularly with a quick jumping one, any such attempt would result in the horse hitting the lady in the face with his head, and thereby thoroughly disgusting her with leaping lessons, to say nothing of possible disfigurement or injury. The instructor cannot be too quiet, simply keeping well hold of his horse, making him walk close to the boards, and cautioning his pupil to sit back—*not away from the crutches* of the saddle, but to throw the upper part of her figure back *the instant the horse drops his head*. Any more instruction will only confuse her. The master should jump with the horse, *but not hold the habit*, as is customary with some preceptors of riding, because no man is so clever on his legs but that some inequality in the tan or turf might cause him to stumble, in which case assuredly he would pull the lady off her horse.

After the first jump the master is better away from both horse and pupil. In nine cases out of ten I have found that the above simple directions to the latter result in her landing all right, except a little derangement of equilibrium to the front; but the easy spring of a well-bred and well-broken horse, and the hold he takes of her hands, reassure her. She has made her *première pas* in jumping, and finds that it is by no means so difficult a matter as she anticipated. In her second attempt, if she exhibits good nerve, as most young ladies of the present day do, the instructor need only walk up the side of the school with her, close to the horse's shoulder, quietly correcting her if she allows her reins to become slack, because in that case she loses the *appui* on the horse's mouth, which in her early attempts at leaping is of vital importance to her. In fact, it is necessary, in order to give the pupil confidence, that the horse should jump with a firm hold upon her hand.

Many authorities on riding tell us that a horse's jump is simply a higher stride of his gallop; from this notion I beg entirely to dissent. In leaping, a horse first raises his forehand upwards with a half rear, both feet quitting the ground at the same instant, the height he rises corresponding to the angle at which he takes off. Secondly, from his hind legs he propels himself forwards, both hind legs moving together, and, if he is a good jumper, well under him. If leaping, therefore, is to be compared to any other action of a horse, it must resemble a plunge gaining ground to the front. There is no possible gain in teaching, however, by comparing a horse's leap to his any other movement. Instinct tells him what to do in order to clear his legs of the obstacle, and, like walking or galloping, the action is by no means artificial, inasmuch as a thoroughly unbroken young horse loose in a paddock will jump through a gap on an ill-kept farm (if his dam makes the running) with precisely the same action as a finished hunter; and, therefore, in one sense I endorse the dictum once expressed to me by an Irish farmer when I asked his opinion as to the natural paces of a horse. His reply was, "Sure some of 'em goes no way natural, but just the way you don't want thim to go; and there's some of thim that nothing's so natural to as to ate a lot of good oats a man never sees the price of again. Thim's bad ones. But if you're spaking of a good maning, rale Irish horse, the most natural pace he has is to jump well." I quite agree, bar the word pace, that jumping to a horse is as natural as any other instinctive action. The weight, however, to be carried, and the mode in which that weight is distributed at the critical moment, makes a material difference to both horse and rider. Therefore, the early leaping lessons should be confined to causing the pupil to do as little as possible to impede the action of the horse, while she preserves her due balance. Like the breaking of a young colt in the case of a pupil learning to ride over a fence, if you ask too much at once or confuse the learner, you obtain nothing but discomfiture.

As regards this portion of the course of equitation, it is specially necessary to bear in mind the old French maxim, *C'est ne pas le première pas qui coute.* At the same time it is quite possible, if the first step is injudiciously taken, to spoil the whole of your previous work. Special care should be taken that the horse does not take off too soon; and if, from any unevenness of the rider's hands or legs, he attempts this, the instructor should be quickly at his head again, and compel him to do his work coolly and collectedly. "The standing leap," as this is technically called, is considerably more difficult as regards catching the precise moment at which to throw the weight of the body back than the "flying leap," because in the standing leap the horse, being nearer to the obstacle, pitches himself forward with a much rougher action, and does not land so far on the other side of the fence; whereas when he canters freely at it, the difference in the shock to the rider is as great as that experienced in the pitch of a boat in a short chopping sea, and the boat's rise and fall in a long swell, the pace also causing the horse to take more freely hold of the rider's hand.

Complete confidence, however, must be established before a lady should be asked to ride her horse at a fence out of a walk; and nearly as much time should be expended over this new step in the series of lessons as were occupied in trotting.

I have not, however, to define the principle upon which, in either standing or flying leap, security of seat must be sought. Some say that in leaping it is by muscular grasp only that a lady can retain her true equilibrium in the saddle; others adhere to the notion that it is all done by balance. Now the truth lies midway between these two theories. It is quite possible for a man to ride over a fence by balance only. Witness what one sees frequently in a circus, where some talented equestrian maintains his footing on a bare-backed steed, while the latter jumps a succession of bars. Here there is nothing to keep the rider on the horse but sheer balance; and, of course, if this can be done by one man standing up, it can be much more easily done by another sitting down in the saddle, although very few men ride across country in such form, nor indeed is it either safe or desirable to do so. The thing, nevertheless, is quite easy. It is not so easy with a lady, because her position on the saddle is altogether an artificial one; and, moreover, the weight of the skirt is sufficient to render riding by balance alone most difficult. It is by a combination of firm grasp on the crutches, *seized* just before the horse arrives at his fence, and a true balancing of the body from the waist upwards, that security of seat in jumping is obtained. A most necessary adjunct to the above, however, is firmness of the arms, because, if the latter are allowed to fly out from the sides, the whole figure becomes, as it were, disconnected, and the proper *aplomb* is lost. By taking a firm hold of the upper crutch of the saddle with the right leg, the rider is enabled to balance her body as the horse rises, while the pressure of the left leg against the third crutch prevents the concussion of his landing from throwing her forward, provided always she throws back her weight at precisely the right moment. This requires practice, and well-timed assistance from the instructor, thus:

As soon as the pupil acquires sufficient confidence to ride her horse fairly up to the fence, and keep his head straight to it, the master should stand far enough from her to obtain a good view of the whole contour of figure of horse and rider. He should place the hands of the latter *well* apart, cause her to shut her fingers firmly on the reins, which give firmness to the body; keep her hands well down and her figure well drawn up, ready on the instant to throw the weight back. He should then caution her to execute the last-named movement on his giving the *single sharp word* " Now." The pupil should then press her horse well up against her hand, and keep his head steady and straight to the bar. The instant he rises the instructor should give his word sharply, and the rider will then catch the true time at which to act upon it. This requires only close attention and watching by instructor and pupil, both being " vif " and thoroughly on the alert. After a few efforts the lady is then sure to find out the time without any word. I have taught a great many very young ladies as well as gentlemen to ride over a fence by the aid of the word given in the above form, and have found it always of the greatest assistance both to myself and pupils. Special attention is necessary to keeping the hands well down and well apart, and the shoulders quite square, because there is a natural tendency on the part of most ladies in the first leaping lessons to throw the right shoulder forward, which not only destroys her balance but causes her to pull the horse's head to the near side. The hands cannot be kept too quiet at first, for any effort to give and take to the action of the horse is nearly certain to result in the pupil checking him at the very moment he springs forward, and pulling him upon his fence.

A well-broken horse, when put up to his bridle, will take a good hold of the rider's hand, and if sufficient length of rein is given him will clear the bar without the necessity of the rider moving her hands a hair's breadth. Subsequently, when she has had sufficient practice to feel quite at home, she can be taught how to assist him when he does a long striding leap over water or a strong double fence with ditches on both sides.

After the standing leap is executed neatly, and in good form by rider and horse, the flying leap should at once be practised.

The pupil should put her horse into a steady canter, going to the left round the school; and for this purpose the hurdle or bar should for the time be removed, so as to enable the lady to get her horse into a good free stride. When the instructor sees that she has her horse in proper form, the hurdle should be put up again and well sloped, because, even so, the horse will jump considerably higher in all probability than the rider expects.

This is the moment at which the master requires to be thoroughly on the alert. He should caution the lady not to let her horse *hurry* when he turns the corner and sees the hurdle, which many horses are very apt to do. " Hands down," " Sit back," " Press him against your hand," and the " Now!" at the right moment should be the concise words, given in a tone at once lively and encouraging. The result will be a clean, clever jump, well done by horse and rider, when the former should be "made much of."

A couple or three leaps so executed are quite enough in a school, because nothing so worries most horses as to keep them continually jumping at the same place, and if the leap is too often repeated, they are apt to sulk or blunder at it.

Within the walls of a good riding house almost every kind of obstacle can be represented which can be met with out of doors. The double, the artificial brook or painted wall, all give the pupil sufficient insight into the form in which a well-taught horse will negotiate any of the fences to be met with in the hunting field; and the lady should be carefully taught how to *stop* and *steady* her horse at a crooked or cramped place.

When once the leaping lessons are commenced, one should be given every day, either before or after the riding out. If the ride is intended to be a long one, the jumping should be done while the horse is fresh, and has all his powers in hand.

When the pupil can do the standing and flying leap, the in and out or double in good form, riding on the snaffle, she should again return to her double bridle, which should be fitted with a curb chain with broad links; and the whole of it should be well padded and covered with soft leather, to prevent any jar upon the horse's mouth in jumping. The reins should be separated and placed as for galloping, the greatest care being taken by the instructor that the curb is no tighter than just to keep it in place, for which a good lip strap should be used, and the curb chain fitted so as to admit the play of quite two fingers between it and the horse's jaw. In placing the reins, the master should see that the greater *appui* is on the snaffle, and that after the pupil closes her hands upon the reins she does not shift her hold of them in the slightest degree. Having now four reins instead of two as formerly, there will be a tendency to " fidget " with them, or obtain a better hold. This must instantly be corrected if it occurs, otherwise ten to one but the lady gets the curb rein too short, and pulls her horse on his fence. At the same time there should be no slack curb rein hanging down, but it should be of such length that, on landing, the horse can just feel the action of the curb, and the reason for this is obvious. In school all leaping may be accomplished on the snaffle; but in the hunting field it is far otherwise. In deep ground a horse requires holding together, and no lady could do this with a snaffle bridle. And, again, in a long run, when a horse has been severely called on, he may make a blunder on landing from a drop in a bit of boggy ground, in which case the curb rein is necessary in aid of the snaffle. As, therefore, it is in the school that the pupil should be prepared for every outdoor eventuality, riding over her fences with both curb and snaffle must be practised; and, finally, over a small jump she must be taught to ride with the curb alone.

CHAPTER XIV.

THE LEAPING LESSON (continued).

It may fairly be accepted as a general rule, that a horse should not be ridden over a fence upon the curb alone. The rule, however, has its exceptions. One of these is the possible case of a lady being placed in such a predicament that she has no alternative in the presence of imminent danger but that of leaping her horse to avoid it, and in such case it may be (and, indeed, in my own experience has occurred) when the lady was riding her horse with a single curb bridle. If the fair equestrian so placed lacks the necessary nerve, dexterity of hand, and firmness of seat, she must come to certain grief. It is therefore highly desirable that, although on ordinary occasions she should use both snaffle and curb in leaping, she should also be thoroughly *au fait* at doing it, if the necessity arises, upon a "hard and sharp," or single "Hanoverian."

Again, leaping on the curb rein only teaches the pupil the full value of every particle of her balance and muscular grasp on the saddle, while it also shows her that, although as a rule a horse requires to be kept well together, there are exceptional instances in which it is necessary to yield the hands freely to him. The above-named is one of these cases. The leaping lessons, however, which lead up to the point of proficiency at which the pupil should be permitted to attempt so critical and difficult a piece of riding must be carefully and inductively given.

Assuming that the fair tyro rides her horse boldly and confidently over the ordinary fences used in a school, and can execute an "in and out" jump without derangement of seat or hand, the effort of the master should next be directed towards teaching his pupil how to cause her horse to extend himself over a jump where there is considerable width as well as height. I must repeat that, for this purpose, a horse should be used that is thoroughly up to his business—one that will stride freely away and *gallop* at his fence. The best practice to begin with, in what I may perhaps call "fast jumping" for a lady, is at an artificial brook.

This is easy enough to arrange in a riding school. It requires only a sheet of canvas, painted the colour of water, of such dimensions that the people in the school can increase or diminish its width at pleasure. This canvas should be long enough to extend from one side of the school to the other, which can be managed by fastening the canvas to a couple of light rollers. On the taking-off side of this artificial brook there should be some low wattles, gorse bound, or otherwise; and these also should extend quite across the school. There is then no chance of a well-broken horse refusing.

Before the canvas arrangement is stretched across the riding-house, the pupil should be instructed to set her horse going at a free striding canter—as fast as is compatible with safety in turning the corners, which should be well cut off in this case, the pupil riding a half-circle at both ends of the school. After two or three turns round the house at this pace, in order to get the horse well into his stride, the assistants should arrange the jump while the instructor prepares his pupil for it. And now let me endeavour to explain the difference in the position and action of the hands of the rider necessary for a long jump as compared with that requisite in a short one. In the latter, safety consists in a horse jumping well together or collectedly, because in a cramped or crooked place speed is almost certain trouble. Where, on the contrary, there is a broad sheet of water to be got over, "plenty of way" on the horse—sufficient speed to give great momentum to his effort, is indispensable. In the short leap or crooked place, then, the horse should be made to jump throughout right into his bridle; and for this purpose the position and steadiness of hand described in the last article, accompanied by such pressure of the leg as will keep him up to it, is the true mode of "doing such places."

But to clear a wide jump, it should be remembered that the horse must not only go a good pace on it, but he must be allowed to extend his head and neck the instant he takes off. If this is neglected, the fair equestrian, in attempting a water jump, will inevitably find herself in the brook.

Now, a man in riding at water has this great advantage over a lady in the same case, that, having equal power with both legs, he can force his horse up to any length of rein, no matter how long, in reason, and compel him to face it, thus enabling the rider to hold him through every inch of his jump, while he gives him plenty of scope to extend himself. For a lady to do this is impossible. Too much pressure of the left leg or repeated use of the spur, even if counteracted on the off side with the whip, would cause the horse to throw his haunches to one side, and he would not jump straight. Steadiness of seat, hand, and leg are therefore indispensable to the lady. The horse ought to be well practised at the particular jump before she is allowed to attempt it, and therefore should require no rousing or urging, to get plenty of way on, for his effort. But before the pupil faces her horse towards the brook, she should be emphatically but quietly enjoined by the instructor to respond to his word "now" as follows: Let it be understood that her elbows should be drawn back until they are three inches or thereabouts behind her waist, the hands about the same distance below the elbows, the former about six inches apart, with the fingers closed firmly on the reins and turned *inwards* and *upwards* until they touch the *waist*, the reins divided, as for galloping, but with the slightest possible feeling upon the curb. With her hands in the above-named form she should ride her horse to his jump, never moving them until she hears the sharp sound of the word "Now!" from the instructor, when at the same instant the body, from the waist upwards, should be thrown back and the hands shot forward, the elbows following, until they are just level with the front of the waist. As the hands go forward, the little fingers should be turned downwards and the knuckles upwards; this will bring the middle joints of both hands with the nails downwards against the right thigh, about four to six inches above (or, as the rider sits, behind) the knee; and this turning down of the nails and forward motion of hands and elbows will give the horse free scope of his head and neck, while the hands coming in contact with the right thigh will still maintain the proper *appui*, and support the horse when he lands in his jump. Although the foregoing appears prolix in description, it occupies little time to explain *vivâ voce*; and with the instructor by her side the lady may practise the action two or three times while her horse is standing still before he faces his jump. The instructor should then quit the lady's side and place himself near the brook in such a position that he has a fair view of the horse as he takes off. The pupil should turn her horse quietly about, and ride to the *left* into the corner of the school, and as soon as the horse's head is square to the jump, and himself square to the boards, the master should give the word smartly, "Canter." With plenty of vivacity, the pupil should immediately strike her horse into a striding pace, keeping her hands well back and hitting him smartly once with the spur. An assistant with a whip should also crack it slightly behind the horse.

Let the master then closely watch the moment at which the horse's fore feet quit the ground, and give his word quickly and sharply, and in nine cases out of ten the jump will be a success.

The artificial brook should be arranged about two-thirds of the distance down the school, so as to give the horse plenty of space to get into his stride before he comes to it, while there will be sufficient room to collect him after he lands. If he does it well the first time (and with the above described handling he will scarcely fail to do so), and the rider performs her part moderately well, the jump should not be repeated. If, however, it is necessary again to go through the instruction, the horse should not be put at the place back again, but the end of the canvas be rolled up and the wattle removed, so as to admit of his passing to the longer reach of the school. These lessons should be given daily until the pupil executes them with the requisite energy and correctness of riding, the instructor taking special care never to ask his pupil, however, to do such jumps unless he sees that she is quite equal in health and good spirits to the occasion. For riding which requires any extra "dash" about it must never be attempted by anybody if they are at all out of nerve.

After the pupil does the brook well, it may be replaced by a double set of gorsed hurdles, placed just so far apart as to necessitate their being done at a single jump. In this case, however, the pupil, while giving her horse by the action of her hands sufficient scope to allow him to jump a considerable distance, should not be allowed to ride so fast at the obstacle, about half the speed necessary to do water being quite sufficient; and the off-side hurdles should be so placed that if the horse strikes them they will give way.

As a rule ladies do not perform, even in Leicestershire, over big double fences, or very strong oxers, and the *indication* of what is required to do them should be sufficient for riding school practice.

As I have elsewhere observed, a horse will jump higher and further when going with hounds than you can with safety ask him to do when in cool blood, or when only roused to extraordinary effort by the use of the spur or whip. And no man in his senses in the hunting field would ever think of piloting a lady to a place which he would only ride at himself at a pinch. Such jumps, therefore, as I have endeavoured to describe within doors should represent the biggest which most ladies are likely to encounter with in a fair hunting country. As regards riding over a fence, with the curb rein unrelieved by the snaffle, the practice should be as follows:

A hurdle should be well sloped, so as to render the leap a very moderate one. The rider should quit her hold of the reins, which should be knotted and fastened by a thong to the mane. A leading rein should then be attached to the ring of the snaffle, and the horse led quietly up to the fence, and halted. The pupil should then draw her hands back until they are in the same position as she would place them in putting her horse at his jump, with the hands closed firmly, which will give steadiness to the body. She must take a determined hold of the upper pommel with her right knee, and be ready with the figure perfectly poised to throw her weight back at the proper moment; placing her left thigh also firmly against the third crutch, her foot well home in the stirrup and well forward, the shoulders perfectly square, and the waist quite pliant. An assistant should then crack a whip smartly in rear of the horse, without hitting him; this will cause him to spring lightly over the hurdle. If the position of the pupil before the horse takes off is carefully looked to, there will be little derangement of seat.

This lesson should be repeated until it is executed with precision. At the same time, two or three jumps of this sort are quite sufficient in one day, because, if repeated too often, the horse, missing the support of the hand, is apt to blunder. When the lady can ride over her fence in the above-named form, she should take up and arrange her reins, so that, while that of the snaffle is not in the horse's way, she feels him on the curb only. She should give him fair length of rein, draw her left hand back to her waist, and place the right hand lightly on the left, just in front of the knuckles; but the reins should be held military fashion—the little finger between them, the leather over the middle joint of the forefinger, the thumb closed firmly on it, the little finger well turned up towards the waist. The horse must be ridden at a smart walk, well up against the curb, until he is close enough to the hurdle to jump. The whip must again be used, and the instructor's word again sharply given, when the pupil should yield both hands freely, turning the little fingers downwards, and slipping the elbows forward. Great firmness and steadiness of seat are necessary to do this lesson well, and considerable practice is necessary to insure complete unity of action in the body and hands, the former being yielded quickly as the latter is actively thrown back. To assist the pupil in her first attempts at this portion of the leaping lesson, the curb chain should be slackened as much as possible, and it should be one that is broad and well padded.

As the lady acquires the requisite lightness of manipulation and additional firmness in the saddle, the curb (link by link) may be tightened until it is in its proper place, namely, so that it admits of the play of one finger only between it and the jaw of the horse. But the greatest care on the part of the instructor is necessary in watching how both horse and rider behave before this can be accomplished.

The lesson is called technically "jumping from the hand," and once thoroughly acquired, the pupil has little to learn, as regards indoor work, in the way of riding over her fences. She may in that respect be considered fit to take her place any time at the covert side, and hold her own, under proper pilotage, with hounds, where of course she will use snaffle and curb reins equally, or according to the temper and breaking of her mount.

During the leaping lessons, and in fact throughout the whole course of equitation up to this point, the pupil should be put upon as many different horses as possible consistent with her progress, care always being taken that she is thoroughly master of one before she is put upon another. The action of horses varies so much in degree, no matter how much from similarity of breed and form it may assimilate in kind, that to attain anything like proficiency the rider's mount requires frequent changing; otherwise, when put upon a strange horse, she would find herself sorely at a loss.

With the exception of one practice, which in some degree resembles the leaping lesson, we may now safely dismiss our fair pupil from technical indoor instruction, except in the way of an occasional refresher, whenever those about her discover any inclination to lapse into a careless form of riding. This both men and women are so apt to do (imperceptibly to themselves), that an occasional sharp drilling does no harm to the most practised rider of either sex.

The final instruction to be given in the school is called the "Plunging Lesson," and may be briefly described as follows, premising that although it is the bounden duty of every man who has anything to do with a lady's riding to avoid by every means allowing her to be put on a restive horse, yet it is always possible that, from some unavoidable cause, a lady (especially in the colonies) may some day find herself on a bad-mannered animal that will "set to" with her. In order, therefore, that in such an undesirable case she may not be at a loss, it is well that when thoroughly practised in leaping, she should be put upon a horse that will kick smartly whenever he is called upon by the master. Such a horse is useful for the above purpose, and is generally to be found in most riding establishments. The trick is easily enough taught, and requires no description. Neither is it at all incompatible with general good manners.

The first thing, then, as regards the pupil, is to impress upon her that whenever a horse "sets to" kicking with her, that her tactics should consist first in keeping his head up, and, secondly, in finding him something else to do than kick.

A horse cannot have his head and his tail up at the same time, therefore, when he kicks, his first effort is to get his head down. This should be immediately counteracted by the rider sitting well back, keeping her hands up as high as her elbows, feeling the horse firmly on the curb reins as well as the snaffle held in one hand, while she applies the whip vigorously across his neck. This will have the effect of causing him to keep his head up and go to the front. The same firm treatment will be successful in most cases where a horse attempts to plunge. But in the latter case the hand must be yielded if there is any attempt to rear, and if the last-named dangerous vice is carried to any length, the rider should not hesitate to take fast hold of the mane, or put her hand in front of the horse's neck. Both rearing or plunging, however, may be effectually prevented by the use of the circular bit and martingale, described under the heading "Rearing Horses and Runaway Dogs" in the *Field* of Nov. 11, 1871. In my humble opinion, every lady going to India and the colonies should have one or two such bits among her outfit of saddlery, and if properly fitted in the horse's mouth, all risk of rearing or even violent flirting is done away with. Such tackle, however, does not prevent a horse from *kicking*, and although no lady should ever attempt to ride one that is possessed habitually of this vice, a sudden accession of kicking may arise in an otherwise good-meaning horse from some ill-fitting of the saddle, or similar casualty, causing tender back or otherwise upsetting him. Of course, no punishment should be resorted to in these cases; but it is as well for a lady to be able to keep her seat in such an emergency, and this she will easily do if she keeps the horse's head up, and her leg well pressed against the third crutch.

On Brighton Downs, some years ago, I saw a young lady thoroughly master a kicking horse in the manner above described, accompanied, however, with a considerable amount of punishment, most resolutely applied with a formidable whalebone whip. No second glance was necessary to perceive that in this case the lady was well aware of the horse's propensity, and had come out for the purpose of thoroughly taking it out of him, which certainly she did effectually, and as he was a vicious-looking weedy thoroughbred, "it served him right."

But I must again enter my protest against ladies running such risks, however accomplished they may be as horsewomen. Let them accept the respectful advice of a veteran, and avoid vicious horses. Brutes that run back, plunge, rear, or kick from sheer vice (and there are many that do) are fit only for the riding of the rougher sex, and only of such of them as have the ill fortune to be compelled to get their living by riding. The so-called plunging lessons above alluded to, however, will give a lady a thorough insight into the orm in which to ride in case of emergency.

CHAPTER XV.

The Hunting Field.

We enter now upon a new and important phase of our pupil's education in the saddle. Before doing so, however, I feel bound to observe that from time to time a vast amount of "twaddle" is ventilated on the question of the propriety of ladies riding with hounds. All sorts of absurd objections have been brought forward against the practice; as, for instance, that hunting as regards ladies is a mere excuse for display and flirtation, and that it is both unfeminine and dangerous. I believe that these objections, made by people who never knew the glorious exhilaration of hunting, may be very briefly disposed of. I reside where the very cream of the midland hunting is carried on, and I perceive that year after year the number of ladies of high rank and social position who grace the field with their presence is on the increase; while to the best of my belief no female equestrians *who are not ladies* have been seen with hounds in Leicestershire or its vicinity for some years. So much for the stamp of woman that hunts nowadays.

As regards flirtation and display, I am at a loss to understand why anti-foxhunting cynics should have selected the covert side, or the road to it, for their diatribes; for there *can* be no time for flirting when hounds are once away. It must be manifest to every man who has the most remote notion of what manner of people our aristocracy and gentry are, that they will only know at the covert side precisely the same stamp of person they meet elsewhere in society. In that society there are dinner parties, flower shows, balls, the opera, all affording equal or better opportunities for flirtation than the hunting field. As to hunting being unfeminine, it is difficult, I submit, to pronounce it any more so than riding in Rotten-row. And finally, as regards danger, I propose to show how it can be rendered all but impossible if due care and forethought are exercised by the male friends or relatives of the hunting lady. Let us now, therefore, having traced out the course of instruction in the riding school, on the road, and in the park, consider how safety is best ensured to the beginner.

As regards the stamp of horse the fair *débutante* of the chase should ride, I have already endeavoured to give my idea. I have only to add that he should be very fit for his work, the pink of condition, without being above himself; and, finally, that no temptation as to fine action or clever fencing should ever induce a lady to ride a hunter that has a particle of vice about him. With the best of piloting it is impossible always to keep her out of a crowd, where she is in a woeful dilemma if mounted on a horse that kicks at others. I have seen this more than once, and have heard expressions from the suffering riders that must have been far from pleasing to refined feminine ears. I must, however, record a special instance of politeness under difficulties which I witnessed during the past season. Hounds were running with a breast-high scent, the pace very fast, when the leading division had their extended front diminished to single file by a big bullfincher, practicable only in one place. Among those waiting their turn to jump was a lady who always rides very forward. She was mounted on a rare-shaped, blood-like animal, that looked all over like seeing the end of a long day, but exhibited considerable impatience at the check. In some cases, as all hunting people know, the difficulty is always increased to those who are compelled to wait by a ruck of riders crowding up from the rear. The case I allude to was no exception to this rule, and among others came a welter middle-aged gentleman, riding a horse quite up to his weight—a grand hunting looking animal, that appeared intent upon clearing every obstacle in his path, not excepting the impatient ones who were doing the gap in Indian file. The veteran, however, who was a capital horseman, managed to pull up his too-eager steed just in rear of the lady's horse, and was forthwith accommodated with a most vicious kick with his near hind leg. Fortunately, the distance was too great to admit of the stout gentleman receiving the full benefit of the intended favour, which nevertheless made his boot-top rattle, and materially altered the genial expression of his rubicund visage. Turning gracefully in her saddle, the fair votary of the chase expressed her deep regret at the bad behaviour of her horse. "I am very sorry—awfully sorry; I hope you are not hurt," she said, in a tone which ought to have consoled any middle-aged sportsman for a broken shin. "I never knew him to do it before," continued the lady. "Pray don't say a word, Miss," replied the old gentleman, taking off his hat with a genuine thoroughbred air; "don't say a word; they are only dangerous when they do it behind." Whether they do it "behind" or "before," kick in a crowd at other horses, or hit at hounds with their fore feet (as some thoroughbreds will do when excited), they are equally disqualified for ladies' hunters, however gaily they may sail over the turf or clear the obstacles in their way.

To proceed with our lessons. Before venturing to take our aspirant for the honours of the chase to a regular meet of foxhounds —where she is apt to become excited, and possibly unnerved by the imposing array of "pink," gallant horsemen, and aristocratic ladies riding steeds of fabulous price, dashing equipages, and thrusting foot people, always ready to embarrass a beginner—it is best to seek out a quiet line nearly all arable land, where the fences will be small, where there are few ditches to be met with, and where the going on the stubble or fallow will be good enough when the crops are off the ground. The pupil should wear a "hunting skirt" properly so called—that is, one not too redundant, made of strong cloth, and booted with leather about eight or ten inches wide round the bottom. This is a very necessary precaution, because it prevents the skirt from hanging up in the fences and getting torn. Hunting boots also should be worn, back-strapped, tongued in at the foot, and reaching nearly to the knee, the upper part made of thick but very flexible leather—buckskin is the best. It is soft, and at the same time thick enough to save the leg from a blow from a strong binder, which occasionally hits very hard in its rebound, having been previously bent forward by somebody who has just jumped the fence.

A "Latchford" spur of the sort before described is also requisite, and the question of the arrangement of skirt necessary to enable the rider to use the spur effectively has caused considerable diversity of opinion among *cognoscenti* on hunting matters. Some ladies have an opening made in the skirt, through which the shank of the spur passes; and in order to keep the latter in its place, it is usual to have a couple of strings strongly stitched on to the inside of the skirt. These are tied round the ankle, and prevent the skirt to a great extent from getting foul of the spur. But this method decidedly involves a certain amount of risk, because, in case of the horse making a blunder and falling, the lady has not the free use of her leg. Again, there is a method of letting the spur shank through a small opening similar to a large eyelet hole, made of strong elastic, and let into the skirt, the point of insertion having been previously measured when the rider is in the saddle and her left leg and foot are properly placed as regards the third crutch and stirrup. But a still better way is that which I have seen adopted lately by several ladies who go very straight with hounds. It is as follows. After the skirt has been carefully measured and *marked* (the lady up), an opening is made perpendicularly, large enough to admit of the lady's foot passing through it. This opening should be made about six or eight inches above the place where the ankle will touch the skirt, when the left leg is fairly stretched down, the knee bent, and the heel sunk. When the instructor has assisted his pupil into the saddle, he should put her foot in the stirrup, and wait until she has carefully arranged her habit; he should then take her foot out again, and the lady should lift it high enough to enable her attendant to pass it *through the opening*. The foot can then be replaced in the stirrup, and the spur buckled on. The upper leather (by the way) should be broad and slightly padded. By these means the left foot and the leg from six to eight inches above the ankle will be entirely clear of the skirt, which will give the rider perfect freedom of action, while the opening is not sufficiently wide to admit of the skirt being blown clear of the leg. This, moreover, is prevented by the leather booting; in fact, in a well-made hunting skirt there should be no slack cloth for the winds to play with at all.

The kind of whip to be used is the crop (without the thong) of a hunting whip; a Malacca crop is the best for a lady, because the lightest. It should have a good crook to it, well roughened on the outside, and be furnished, moreover, with a roughened nail head, in order to prevent the crop slipping when the rider attempts to open a gate. Gauntlet gloves with strong leather tops are best, because they prevent the possibility of the rider's hands being scratched or injured in jumping a ragged fence; but if the lady dislikes gauntlets, the sleeve of the jacket should be made to fasten with three buttons close to the wrist, because the sleeves now so much in fashion, being very wide at the wrist, are apt in taking a fence to catch and get torn, in addition to the risk of the rider being pulled off her horse. These casualties, which of course cannot occur with the clean-made jump taken in the riding school, are likely enough to happen in the field, and should be carefully guarded against.

As regards the shape and make of the jacket I have already said so much, that I must leave it to the taste and figure of the rider, always assuming that while she allows herself plenty of freedom of movement, she does not wear anything too loose, or any *steel* supports about her, as for hunting these are highly dangerous.

As regards headgear, the same style of thing that sufficed for the riding school may not be considered sufficiently effective for the hunting field; and, without venturing upon ground so delicate as an opinion or even knowledge of ladies' "coiffure," I may say that at Melton and other fashionable hunting centres there has for some time existed an artful combination between the ladies' hat makers and the hair dressers, by means of which that very elegant affair the "Melton hat" is deftly fitted with an arrangement of hair behind which is immovable, no matter where the wearer jumps in hunting. The hairdresser's services are first called into requisition; possibly he imparts the "arcana" of his craft to the lady's maid; but one or other succeeds in making such an arrangement of the hair as renders it at once secure in riding and becoming to the style of the lady herself. The hat with the hair attached behind is then placed on the head, and secured by an invisible elastic band. Should any of my readers desire information on these matters, so important to a lady's comfort in the hunting field, I can furnish them with the names of the people in Melton and elsewhere who can give them every detail.

Having our pupil accoutred as before described, and taken her to a quiet farm, the instructor should pick out a line, start at a walk in front of his charge, pop his horse quietly over the fences, and see that his pupil does them with equal coolness and without rush or hurry. When she can do this well, the pace should be increased to a steady canter; and the master riding beside her should be careful that she *steadies* her horse three or four lengths before he takes off, always riding him well into the bridle.

This kind of practice should be continued for some days, until the pupil is quite at home at her work, and the master should then proceed to instruct her as to the mode in which to make her horse "crawl" through gaps and crooked, cramped places, and do "on and off" jumps and doubles. The animal best adapted for this sort of practice is one that is *clever* rather than *fast*. An Irish horse, out of a ditch and bank country, is preferable. But the instructor should take special care, by first doing these "on and off" jumps himself, to ascertain that the banks are sound; otherwise there is danger of just the worst kind of fall a woman can have. We have lately had a lamentable instance of this in the case of a noble lady, one of the most brilliant horsewomen in England.

For my own part, I am entirely against a lady jumping her horse in the field at any place where there can be the slightest doubt as to good foothold, unless she is preceded by a man to pilot her. If the latter gets down, he can always (assuming him to be a good workman) get clear of his steed, whereas at these rotten places a lady and her horse are likely to fall "all of a heap," and injury greater or less is a certainty to the rider.

Not long since I saw a little girl, about ten years old, riding with hounds on a mite of a pony which was as clever as a monkey. The little heroine took a line of her own (no doubt she knew the country well), and kept her place among the foremost for some time; presently she disappeared, and we found her impounded, pony and all, up to the back of the latter in a piece of rotten ground which had let them in like a "jack in the box." Neither the pony nor his plucky little rider were hurt, but (as they say in Ireland) that was more by good luck than good guiding.

I maintain that children at that age should never be left in the hunting field to their own devices, however well they may ride, and that, either in their case or that of young ladies of riper age, they should never be allowed to go with hounds, unless accompanied by a man who is not only a thorough horseman and judge of hunting, but is also well acquainted with the country he is riding over, and accustomed to pilot ladies.

After the pupil has learned to make her horse "creep" in the manner above described—to insure success in which, however, the closest watching is necessary on the part of the instructor, and directions requisite in each individual case, utterly impossible in written general instructions—she should be carefully taught to open gates for herself, because it is nearly sure hereafter to occur that she may have to ride at a pinch in a country place where her route lies through a line of bridle gates, and the attendance of a man to open them for her may not be available. Nothing is easier than for a lady to open a well-hung and well-latched gate, the hinges of which are on the off side. Bridle gates occur most frequently in great grazing countries, such as Leicestershire, Warwickshire, or Northamptonshire, by reason of the necessity of confining cattle within certain limits. The gates are generally heavy, well poised on their hinges, and opening either with wooden latching or iron spring ones, easily reached at the top.

If the gate is hung on the off side, all the lady has to do is to ride her horse with his head in an oblique direction between the gatepost and the gate, so that when she has the latter open she can continue moving on in the same slanting direction. She should first press the end of her crop down upon the latch, if it is a wooden one, keeping herself perfectly upright in the saddle, and steadily seated in it. Directly the latch lifts she should press firmly against it with the rough crook, push the gate open, and press her horse onwards in the same oblique direction, by which the animal's croup clears the gate sooner, and all risk of its closing on him is avoided. If there is a long iron spring latch to the gate, it must first be pulled open with the crop, so that the latch rests against the hasp, and a steady purchase must then be taken against the upper bar with the crop, and the gate thus quietly pushed forward : this if it opens *from* the rider. If the reverse, the horse's head should be kept perfectly square close to the gate post, until the latch is lifted and rested on the hasp. The gate should then be *pulled* open, and the horse's head inclined just the reverse way to that adopted when the gate opens *from* the rider. But in no case should she *lean* forward, or put herself out of her balance, in order to get hold of the latch or the gate itself, and she should be particularly careful that the reins do not catch against the long iron hasps so common to the gates I speak of.

Only last year, I met a lady who rides a good deal unattended and, seeing her about to open a gate I knew to be rather an awkward one, I trotted on to assist her; but (possibly desiring to show me that she could do it unassisted) she leant forward to give the gate *a lift*, and in doing so she dropped the reins upon her horse's neck, when the animal immediately hooked the headstall of a single curb bridle upon a long iron hasp, and, finding himself fast to it, drew back suddenly and broke the headstall, the bit fell out of his mouth, and the lady (utterly helpless) had no alternative but to slip off as quickly as possible. Fortunately, the animal was a very quiet one, or the consequences might have been serious; as it was, we managed to change bridles, and, having spliced the broken one, went on our separate ways. But, I repeat, one cannot be too careful or methodical in opening gates. When one opens from the *near* side, the reins must be passed into the right hand, the crop into the left, and the greatest care taken, if the gate opens *to* the rider, to *push it* well back behind the horse's quarters before she moves on, riding with her horse's head *towards the hinges*. When a near-side hung gate opens *from* the rider, there is less difficulty, it being only necessary after lifting the latch to push against the gate with the crop, sitting quite upright, and giving swing enough to the gate to enable the rider to get clear of it. But in either case, to or from, with a gate hung on the near side the latch should first be lifted, by using the crop in the *right hand*, resting the

K

latch if possible against the hasp, and then changing hands with the crop and reins as before mentioned. If this is not done, and the rider attempts to lift the latch with her left hand, she must change the direction of her horse's head when the gate is open, at the great risk of bringing it on his quarters.

These directions, like others I have ventured upon, may appear too minute; but it should be remembered that, whereas, carefully followed out, a lady on a steady horse accustomed to gates can open them with safety, any carelessness may result in a bad accident, because the steadiest horse, if "hung up" in a gate, will become furious if he cannot instantly get clear of it. When, therefore, the pupil is well practiced at this sort of work, and has learned to feel her way in cramped places as well as to do her fences at a steady canter, a fair half-speed gallop may be ventured on, the pupil setting her horse going, and pressing him if necessary with the spur, to take his fences in his stride, the spur being used, however, some distance from the fence. The master should ride beside his pupil in this lesson, carefully watching the pace of the horse and the action of the rider. A nice easy line of about a couple of miles should be taken, and the pace maintained throughout. A month of this kind of practice will form a capital introductory step to hunting: and when, in the mild misty mornings of russet-brown October, foxhounds begin to beat up the quarters of the vulpine juveniles, abjuring her "beauty sleep," the lady may with advantage, before the "early village cock proclaims the dawn," don her hunting habiliments, and, under the careful tutelage of her "pilot," trot off to covert and see the "beauties" knock the cubs about.

This is by far the best way to begin hunting in reality. There are very few people about at that early hour, and those only who are thorough enthusiasts about the sport; consequently there is more time for the new votary of Diana to get accustomed to the alteration in her horse's form of demeaning himself. For be it known to the uninitiated that even an old horse, that requires kicking and hammering along a road when ridden alone, is quite a different animal and mover the instant he sees the hounds, and will show an amount of vivacity perhaps very little expected by his rider;

while a well-bred young one requires a great deal of riding on such occasions.

The short bursts sometimes obtained in "cub hunting" are capital practice for a lady; while occasionally a veteran fox, some wily old purloiner of poultry, affords a good twenty or five-and-twenty minutes, even when the fences are blind. I recommend our pilot, however, to keep his charge out of these latter matters, for blind jumping is always bad for a lady.

As regards taking a beginner out with harriers, I am against it. It is very well for invalids or corpulent gentlemen who are " doing a constitutional;" but it teaches a young lady nothing of what is really meant by hunting—which, however, she is in a first-rate position to learn with the cubs.

Staghunting with a deer turned out from a cart and caught with a whipthong, is equally inefficacious, because the hunting as a rule only commences when the run is over. Moreover, there is always a crowd of people who come out for riding only, and care nothing about hunting, and these are the most likely to get into a lady's way, and bring her to grief.

The same may be said of drag hunting, which I hold to be no place for a lady, any more than steeplechasing.

Let us then, legitimately to inaugurate our pupil into the usages and forms of hunting proper, stick to cub hunting until November opens the fences and gives her a chance to prove the value of her previous instruction.

Before closing this article, I cannot refrain from citing an instance of the great value of a lady learning to cross the country well, irrespective of the sport of foxhunting and its health-giving and exhilarating effects. Within ten miles of where I write this resides a lady, young, wealthy, and beautiful, who, although not a religious *recluse*, is as thorough and sincere a devotee of religion as any cloistered nun. Her whole time is spent in acts of charity, and ministering to the spiritual and bodily welfare of the poor for miles round her residence. No weather is too inclement, no night too dark, to stop her on her errands of mercy and charity. If summoned even at the dead of night to attend the bedside of a sick or dying person, as frequently happens, she will dress herself quickly in rough habiliments suitable to it—maybe in tempestuous weather —saddle and bridle a horse herself if her people are not quick enough for her, and, provided with cordials, a prayer book, and a long hunting crop, she will gallop off the nearest way to her destination, taking the fences, if they lie in the road, as they come; and one bright moonlight night I saw her do two or three places that would stop half the men that ride to hounds hereabouts. This lady, who may fairly and without exaggeration be called the "ministering angel" of the district, does not, it is true, hunt now; but it was in riding to hounds that she acquired her wonderful facility of getting over the country.

The above is no sensational story. The lady, her brilliant riding, her true religion, and her charities, are well known, and can be vouched for by hundreds of people in this part of the world. Who shall say after this that hunting is unfeminine?

I have a word more to add, according to promise, as regards the fitting of the circular bit.

This bit, which can always be procured at Messrs. Davis's, saddler, 14, Strand, is fitted in the horse's mouth above the mouthpiece of a snaffle or Pelham bridle. It has a separate headstall, and is put on before the ordinary bridle. It requires no reins, is secured by a standing martingale to a breastplate, and is a certain remedy for horses flirting or rearing when too *fresh* (which, however, I repeat, for a lady's riding should never be allowed).

The strap between the breastplate and the ring bit should be just long enough to enable the horse to move freely forward, without liberty enough to admit of his rearing.

In the next chapter I will endeavour to describe what regular hunting for a lady means; point out the readiest way of getting to our most fashionable packs of hounds; and how ladies residing even in the metropolis may enjoy a day or two of good sport on this fine grass country at the least necessary expense, may witness and enjoy hunting in its perfection, and, if requisite, may breakfast in Mayfair or Belgravia, have a glorious gallop over the Midland pastures, and return to a late dinner. Of course I am aware that neither of the above-named localities is likely to hold many hunting ladies in November. But the fashionable quarters of London are not deserted in February, and spring hunting is perhaps after all the most enjoyable.

CHAPTER XVI.

The Hunting Field (*continued*).

AMONG the many advantages afforded by the "iron road" to lovers of hunting there is none more appreciable than the facility it affords to those who reside in a non-foxhunting country of getting to hounds with ease and rapidity.

Without any greater inconvenience than the necessity of early rising, a lady who lives in Tyburnia or Belgravia may easily enjoy a day's hunting in Warwickshire or Leicestershire, and be in her own home again in reasonable time in the evening.

During the early spring hunting of the present year, several ladies came to Market Harborough and Melton on these sporting expeditions, and returned the same day thoroughly satisfied.

One party, consisting of three ladies and as many gentlemen, seemed to me to have been admirably organised, and to be quite a success throughout.

They left Saint Pancras at eight o'clock in the morning, in a saloon carriage, arrived at Melton at half-past ten, and were at the meet at eleven, with military punctuality. They enjoyed a capital day with the Quorn hounds, left Melton at half-past six, after riding a considerable distance back, and arrived in town at nine o'clock.

A novel and agreeable feature in the arrangement was that the party dined in their luxurious carriage while being whirled back to the metropolis, a first-class dinner and the best of wines having been furnished from the hotel, and served in admirable form. After the journey and the sport one of the ladies (I was told) held a numerously attended and fashionable reception at her own house the same evening; and with a brougham in waiting at St. Pancras, and a pair of fast horses, joined to the wonderful "smartness" (if I may be permitted the expression) displayed by the fair and aristocratic votary of Diana in the field, I should think the thing quite possible as regarded time.

The above-named party was mounted at Melton by some friends; but, by giving fair notice, thoroughly good and well-made hunters can always be secured by any of the Midland hunting centres by those who do not care to rail their own horses from London. Market Harborough is still more accessible than Melton, being but two hours from London, and situated in the centre of a splendid grass country, hunted by Mr. Tailby; while a smart trot of eight miles would bring the sporting *voyageur* to Kilworth Sticks and the Pytchley, provided the right day was selected. Rugby, too, is equally accessible, and boasts a fair hotel, where the charges are not more extortionate than they are at Harborough, which is saying a good deal. The hunting in the vicinity of Rugby, however, amply compensates for a little overdoing in the matter of charges.

It is scarcely possible to go to Rugby the wrong day to get at hounds within a reasonable distance, and some of the meets of that admirable pack, the North Warwickshire, are frequently at such picturesque and convenient trysting places as Bilton Grange—now celebrated by the Tichborne trial, and sworn to as the place where the "Claimant" was not. However this may be, a straight-necked and wily gentleman is generally to be found at home, either in the plantations of the grand old demesne or close by at Bunker's Hill or Cawston Spinney, who is tolerably certain to lead the claimants for his brush a merry dance across the glorious grass country to Barby, Shuckborough, or Ashby St. Leger. The fences, too, in this part of the Midlands are just the thing for a lady's hunting, and, while quite big enough in most cases to require a little doing, they are by no means so formidable as those in High Leicestershire and the Quorn country. The old-fashioned bullfincher is rare, and double ox fences equally so, while there is a pretty variety of nice stake-and-binders, pleached hedges, and fair-water jumping, with an occasional flight of rails, big enough to prove that the fair equestrian's hunter can do a bit of timber clean and clever. In fact, I know no country I would as soon select for a young lady to commence regular hunting in as that in the vicinity of Rugby. Combe Abbey, Misterton, and Coton House are all sweetly English, as well as thoroughly sporting places of meeting, and the truly enjoyable trot or canter over the springy turf, which everywhere abounds by the roadside in these localities, and makes the way to covert so pleasant, has more than once been pronounced by hunting critics to be more desirable than hunting itself in parts of England where the road is all "Macadam," and the land plough, copiously furnished with big flint stones, such as one sees in Hampshire. *Apropos* of which charming country there is a sporting tale prevalent in this real home of the hunter.

A rich, middle-aged, single gentleman, a thorough enthusiast about foxhunting, had a nephew, a very straight-going youngster, who the "prophetic soul" of his uncle had decided should one day be *the* man of the country in the hunting field, and second to none over our biggest country; and, to enable "Hopeful" to lead the van, the veteran mounted him on horses purchased regardless of expense. Furthermore, determined that no casualty in the way of breaking his own neck should suddenly deprive his favourite nephew of the golden sinews of the chase, the old Nimrod made a very proper will, leaving all his large property to his fortunate young relative.

Things, indeed, looked rosy enough for our young sportsman. Youth, health, wealth, a capital seat, and fine hands upon his horse, any quantity of pluck, a thorough knowledge of hunting, and plenty of the best horses to carry him—who could desire more? Alas that it should be so! even the brightest sunshine may become overcast—the fairest prospect be marred—by causes never dreamt of by the keenest and most far seeing among us.

At the termination of a capital season in the Midland, our youngster, not content to let well alone, and, like that greedy boy Oliver still "asking for more," unknown to his worthy uncle, betook himself to the New Forest in Hampshire.

"Hopeful" was a sharp fellow enough, and he did not believe that all was gold that glittered; but he was under a very decided impression that wherever there was a good open stretch of green level turf it was safe to set a horse going." Alas! the luckless young sportsman was not aware that in the New Forest this is by no means a certainty, and one day, when riding to some staghounds, determined to "wipe the eye" of the field, he jumped a big place which nobody else seemed to care for, and, taking his horse by the head, set him sailing along the nearest way to the hounds. A lovely piece of emerald-green turf was before him; he clapped his hat firmly on, put down his hands, and, regardless of wild cries in his rear, made the pace strong. Suddenly and awfully as the Master of Ravenswood vanished from the sight of the distracted Caleb Balderstone and was swallowed up in the Kelpie's Flow, so disappeared "Hopeful" and his proud steed; both were engulfed in a treacherous bog, and, before either horse or man could be extricated, "the pride of the Shires" was smothered in mud beneath his horse.

Next season, at a "coffee-housing" by a spinney side, where hounds were at work, an old friend of the bereft uncle ventured to condole with him on his loss.

"Sad business," he said, shaking his old hunting chum warmly by the hand; "sad business that about poor Charlie down in Hampshire!"

"Sad, indeed," replied the veteran uncle, returning the friendly squeeze. "Who would have thought my sister's son would have ever done such a thing? Staghunting was bad enough," he continued, as the irrepressible tear coursed down his furrowed cheek; "staghunting was bad enough, but to go at it in Hampshire—I shall never get over it. As to his being smothered, of course that served him perfectly right."

Turning, however, from the above melancholy instance of degeneracy in sport to the pleasanter theme of the right locale in which a lady should commence foxhunting, I must not forget Leamington, the neighbourhood of which beautiful and fashionable watering place affords some capital sport to those who delight in "woodland hunting." The woods at Princethorpe, Frankton, and the vicinity, hold some stout foxes that afford many a nice gallop, while the country is rideable enough for a lady if she keeps out of the woods.

Leamington, too, has first-rate accommodation for hunting people. There are, indeed, no better hotels to be met with anywhere than the "Regent" or the "Clarendon," or more moderate charges for first-class houses; while the "Crown" and the "Bath" afford capital quarters for gentlemen, and ample provision for doing their horses well.

The charming Spa, moreover, is at an easy distance from Rugby, and by railing a horse to the latter place, ready access can be had to hunting in the open country, six days in the week.

My advice, then, to young ladies, who desire to witness foxhunting in perfection, is to select one of the above-named localities, and to put herself at once under the guardianship in the field of a thoroughly good pilot who knows the country.

Words of advice to the latter are superfluous. All the men who undertake the responsible office of guiding a lady after hounds hereabouts are quite at home at their business, and it may be satisfactory to my fair readers to know, that, although there are a great number of ladies riding regularly with hounds in the North Warwickshire, Pytchley, and Atherstone country, no accident attended with injury to a lady rider has occurred within my recollection, which extends over a long series of years.

The initiation at cub hunting will have given our pupil confidence, and accustomed her to the excitement shown more or less by every horse at the sight of hounds; and careful attention to the rules of jumping before laid down will insure safety if she adheres carefully to her pilot's line. It is as well, however, that she should understand wherein consists the reason for what her hunting guide does, and what should be done and left undone, from the time of arrival at the meet until the *retour de chasse*.

In the first place, then, while her mentor will of course see to her girths and horse appointments before a start is made to draw a covert, the lady should carefully look to her own dress, head gear, &c., and be certain that everything is in its place, and shows no signs of giving way. But if anything chances to be out of order—

if she has ridden to the meet any considerable distance—it is best to dismount and repair damages at once. As a rule, there are always houses available for this, and nimble-fingered dames zealous in the service of any lady who desires their assistance.

When the fair votary of the chase travels to the meet on wheels, I recommend her by all means the use of a warm overcoat, of which the Ulster is very convenient, and was very much worn for the above purpose last season. In proceeding from the meeting place to the covert a great thing is to keep out of the crowd—no matter how well-behaved a horse the rider may be on—because in a ruck there is always more or less danger of her being kicked herself. The most likely position for a good start will of course be selected by the pilot; but it should be remembered that to be quiet while hounds are at work in covert is a fixed law of the hunting code; to avoid heading a fox when he breaks away, another vital point; and no exclamation of surprise or wonder should be allowed to escape the lips, even if a fox (as I have seen happen more than once) should run between the horses' legs. Foxes, though it may be assumed that they all possess a large amount of craft and cunning, differ as much in nerve and courage as other animals; and while one will sometimes dash through a little brigade of mounted people, the shout of a small boy on foot may turn him back; and while Reynard, again, will frequently rush off close to a lady's horse and take no notice of either him or his rider if both remain quiet, the waving of a handkerchief, or even the slightest movement of the lady on her steed, may cause Sir Pug to alter his mind, and thus a good thing may be spoilt. For the foregoing reasons, therefore, to be perfectly quiet and remain steady, if near a possible point at which a fox can break away, is indispensable. When hounds are settling on his track great care should be taken to avoid getting in their road, or in any way interfering with them. After they have settled, the object should be to *go well to the front and keep there*—first, because the greatest enjoyment in hunting, viz., seeing the hounds work, is by that means attained; and, secondly, whenever there is a check, a lady riding well forward gets all the benefit of it for her horse, whereas those who lose ground at the start, and have to follow on the line, keep pounding away without giving their horses a chance of catching their wind—a very material thing in a quick run.

A check of a few minutes, affording a good horse time, has enabled many a one to stay to the end of the longest run, when an equally good animal has been "pumped" in the same thing for want of such a respite from his exertions.

Again, a great point to be observed is to maintain such a position as will enable the rider to turn with the hounds at the right moment; resolutely resisting any temptation in order to cut off ground, to turn too soon, and risk spoiling sport by crossing their line.

It should be remembered that it is quite as easy to jump the fences when one is in the front rank, as it is when sculling along with the rear guard, and much safer, because the ground always affords better foothold and landing, when it has not been poached up by a number of people jumping. This is especially the case after a frost, when the going is at all greasy.

Even in cases when hounds slip an entire field, and get the fun all to themselves, still those who get away well at first will have all the best of the "stern chase."

If, fortunately, our fair tyro is well up when a fox is run into and killed, she should carefully avoid getting too close to the hounds when they are at their broken-up prey. There are always keen eyes about that can discern on these occasions whether a lady has been riding straight and well, and there will not be wanting some gallant cavalier to offer her the tribute due to her "dash" and good workmanship, in the shape of that coveted trophy of the chase, the brush. There may, however, be more than one lady up on these occasions (I have seen several after very good things), and, as a rule, the brush is most likely to be offered to the lady of the highest rank. These trophies, therefore, are scarcely to be counted upon as a reward for even the best and straightest riding—the less so as of late years it has been observed that in most cases a very stout and straight-necked fox succeeds in eluding his pursuers, and "lives to fight another day."

In beginning regular hunting, one good run in a day for a lady should suffice for some little time. In November the days are very short, and often enough a fox started after three o'clock will be running strong when darkness comes on. For a lady, and a beginner especially, it is best to leave off and trot quietly home while there is yet daylight.

As regards "get up" or equipment, I must add to my former suggestions that a lady for the hunting field should be provided always with a waterproof overcoat, which should be rolled up in as small a compass as possible, and is better carried by her pilot or her second horseman (if she has one out) than attached by straps to the off-side flap of her own saddle; as, in addition to spoiling the symmetry of the saddle on that side, I have seen instances of things so attached hanging up in ragged fences, no matter how carefully they may have been put on.

A sandwich case and flask are highly necessary also. Hunting is a wonderful promoter of appetite, and it is not beneficial to a young lady's health to go from early breakfast to late dinner time without refreshment; while it is quite possible—nay, very probable in a grass country—that she may be a long way from head-quarters when she leaves the hounds, and in a part where refreshment for a lady cannot be had for love or money.

The Melton people have met this requirement very efficiently. Thus, into a very flat, flexible flask, with a screw-cup top, they put a most succulent liquid, composed of calves' foot jelly and sherry. This flask is accompanied by a very neat little leather case, which contains half a dozen nice biscuits, or, in some instances, a small pasty, composed of meat. These cases, with the flask, are made to fit into the pocket of the saddle on the off-side under the handkerchief, and the flap of the pocket is secured by a strap and buckle.

To roll a waterproof neatly, the following plan is the best: Lay the garment down flat, opened out, on a table, the inside upwards; turn the collar in first, then turn the sleeves over to the inside, laying them flat; next turn in both sides of the coat from the collar downwards, about eight or ten inches; then turn in the bottom of the garment about the same distance, when it will form a pocket.

One person should hold this steady while another rolls the collar end very tightly up towards the pocket; it will then fit into it so closely as to make a very small and compact roll of the whole coat.

I must not omit to say that, in addition to the first-rate hunting to be had in the Midlands, there is some good sport with hounds obtainable nearer the metropolis, namely, in the Vale of Aylesbury, with that noble patron of sport, Baron Rothschild. But still I must award the palm to Leicestershire, Warwickshire, and Northamptonshire as far away superior to anything in the hunting way to be seen in any other part of England. In whatever part, however, the fair lover of hunting seeks her sport, she should bear in mind that when she is once away with hounds she cannot be too particular as to riding her horse with the utmost care and precision, and to avoid taking liberties with him by jumping big places for the sake of display. It cannot be too strenuously impressed upon her mentor that, as long as the true line to the hounds can be maintained, the less jumping that is done, the longer the horse will last; that one big jump takes as much out of him as galloping over three big fields; and that he should be *ridden every inch of the way*, because when hounds get off with a good scent it is impossible to say that they may not keep on running for a couple of hours, in which case, if too much is done with him at first, he will inevitably, to use a racing phrase, "shut up."

The light weight of most hunting ladies is a point in favour of the horse; but it is more than counterbalanced by the absence of support which a man who rides well can give with the right leg. It is the absence of this support in the case of a lady's horse, however well ridden, that causes him to tire sooner than he would if ridden by a gentleman; and hence the necessity in selecting a horse to carry a woman with hounds for having not only staying power, but two or three stone in hand. Nevertheless, although unable to give to the animal as much help as can be afforded by a gentleman, ladies can do much by the exercise of that tact and judgment which is their peculiar gift.

Every lady who hunts is sure to be more or less an enthusiast about horses, and is always, according to my experience, ready to adopt any suggestion which tends to their well doing. I therefore venture to point one or two matters which I trust will be found useful.

In the first place, when the hounds have settled to their fox and people have shaken themselves into their places, the fair rider in her early essays in the field should bestow her principal attention upon the animal, upon which depends much of her sport. With a good man by her side, she will run no risk from thrusting neighbours, and although she cannot too soon begin to have "one eye for the hounds and another for the horse," it is the latter which demands all her energies. The whole business is exciting. The genuine dash, the vigour, the reality, that is so striking to a novice when hounds come crashing out of covert, through an old wattle, or bounding over a strong fence; the up-ending and plunging of impatient young horses, the brilliant throng of fashionable equestrians, the rattle of the turf under the horses' feet as they stride away—all these, or any of them, are quite sufficient to warm up even old blood, and are certain to send that of the young going at such a pace that all rule and method in riding is very apt to be forgotten, or thrust aside in the eager desire "to be first."

It is just at this critical moment that I would advise my fair readers to lay to heart the necessity of controlling their excitement, because it is at such a time that a horse, especially at the beginning of the season (if allowed), will "take out of himself" just what he will want hereafter, assuming a stout fox that means business to be to the front. A soothing word or two, and "making much" of the excited steed, will generally cause him to settle in his stride and cease romping; whereas, if the rider is excited as well as the horse, we have oil upon fire at once. Again, it cannot be too forcibly impressed upon ladies riding with hounds that the latter require *plenty of room to work*.

"Place aux dames" is a rule rigidly observed by gentlemen in the hunting field. Room for the hounds should form an equally inviolable law with ladies in the same place. And it is the more necessary to impress this upon beginners, because many a first-rate man who pilots ladies, although bold as a lion over a country, and cautious to a degree as to the line he takes for his fair *compagnon de chasse*, is oftentimes far too modest to check her exuberant riding, and the consequence is, many an anathema—not loud, but deep—is bestowed upon both by exasperated masters and huntsmen.

Unlike the professional riding master, a first-rate pilot—such, I mean, as is paid for his services—though well behaved and respectful, is likely enough to lack much education, except such as he has received in the saddle or on practical farming matters; and his awe of a lady, properly so called, is so considerable as to preclude his exercise of the *fortiter in re* altogether, no matter how much his charge is unwittingly infringing the rules of sport.

I saw an amusing instance of this not long ago. A lady, the widow of a wealthy civil servant in India, having returned to her native land laden with the riches of the East, being still young and excessively fond of riding, purchased a stud of first-class hunters, took a nice little hunting box in Leicestershire for the season, and engaged the services of a very good man to pilot her. As a rule every lady rides in India—some of them ride very well; but a rattling gallop at gun fire, in the morning, over the racecourse at Ghindee or Bangalore, is quite a different matter to a gallop with the Pytchley hounds. The "Bebe sahib" (great lady) had no idea, mounted as she was, of anybody or anything (bar the fox) being in front of her. And be it known to those who have never been in India that "great ladies" there are "bad to talk to," being in the habit pretty much of paying very little attention to anything in the way of counsel coming from their subordinates. Our Indian widow was no exception. So she did all sorts of outrageous things in the field in riding in among the hounds—and, indeed, before them—to the disgust of the master and everybody else, including her pilot, who in her case was certainly no mentor—but the latter was too well paid to risk offending the peccant lady; he ventured a gentle hint or two, and, being snubbed, gave it up for a bad job.

He was so severely rated, however, by the masters of hounds in the district—one of whom declared he would take them home directly he saw the lady and her pilot with them—that the latter was fairly at his wits' end to know how to keep the too dashing widow within bounds. Sorely puzzled, he sat in his spacious chimney nook one night smoking his pipe in moody silence, his wife knitting opposite him.

"What's the matter, John?" began his spouse. "Matter!" he replied; "it's enough to drive a man mad; Mrs. Chutnee's going again to-morrow, and, as sure as fate, she'll ride over the hounds or do something, and get one into trouble."

"What makes her go on so, John?" again inquired the *cara sposa*.—"Go on! it is go on: I think that the name for it. Go on over everything! no fence is too big for her. I like her for that, but she never knows when to stop. Last week she knocked an old gentleman over, and he lost a spick span new set of teeth as cost, I dare say, a matter of twenty guineas; and the day before yesterday she lamed a hound as was worth a lot of money, to say nothing of hurting the poor brute. I don't know what to be at with her, and that's a fact, because, barring her going so fast, she is the best-hearted lady ever I see."

And John relapsed into silence, blowing mighty clouds of smoke, while his wife plied her knitting-needles. But a woman's wit, in difficult cases, is proverbial; and in the watches of the night a bright notion, based upon knowledge of her own sex, flashed upon the anxious mind of the snoring John's wife. The result was as follows. Next morning, true to time, John was in attendance to accompany the fair widow to the field. They had some distance to ride to covert, and after a smart spurt of a mile or two on the sward, the lady pulled her horse up to walk up a hill.

"John," said the lady (who was in high spirits), "what do people here think of my riding?"—"Well, some thinks one thing, and some thinks another," was the reply.

"That's no answer," observed the fair interlocutor; "what do they say? that is the thing. I know one thing they can't say; none of them can say they can stop me over any part of the country, no matter how big it is."

Opportunity, says some wise man, is for him who waits. Now was John's opportunity to avail himself of his clever little wife's bright idea.

L

"Stop you, my lady! no, that's just what they do all say; and what's more, they say you can't stop yourself—that you ain't got no hands, and your horse takes you just where he pleases, if it's even right over the hounds."

The "Bebe sahib" was bitterly chagrined, for she prided herself justly upon her capital hands upon a horse. She was silent for a few minutes, and then she said, "I want you to tell me what to do, just to let these people know, as you do, that I have hands."— "Then I will tell you," my lady, said John, brightening up. "Just you do this: when the hounds get away, you let me go first, and keep your horse about a hundred yards behind me. I'll pick out a line big enough, I'll warrant, and that will show them all about your seat and your jumping. Then about the hands; if you please, whenever I pull up, you do the same. They say as you can't stop your horse, you know."

"Can't I?" said the little lady, "can't stop my horse when I like! I'll let them see that. Can't stop! I should like to know what a woman can't do if she makes up her mind to do it."

John's wife was a capital judge; there was no more riding over hounds or disarranging of elderly gentlemen's teeth. But the "Bebe sahib" has taken me to the extremity of my space, and I must pull up, reserving further observations and suggestions on the hunting field for my next chapter.

CHAPTER XVII.

The Hunting Field (*continued*).

On reading my previous observations on Fox-hunting, it may occur to many ladies that in order to enjoy the sport, great nerve and physical power, as well as a thorough knowledge of the principles of equitation and long practice, are indispensable, and that in default of either of the above qualifications they ought not to venture into the field. This, however, would be an extreme view of the case. It is quite true that to go straight to hounds and take the country and the fences as they come it is necessary that a lady should be in vigorous health, as well as a thoroughly accomplished horsewoman. But, grant the latter condition, those of even more delicate constitutions, and consequently lacking the nerve and strength to take a front-rank place and keep it, may still participate to a great extent in all the enjoyable and healthy excitement of the chase, if they follow it out in a grass country), and put themselves under the guidance of a man who knows that country well.

It cannot be too generally known to those who are not strong enough to sail away with the hounds over big fence or yawning brook that one great advantage as regards hunting afforded by a grass country is that a lady who is attended by a man well up at the topography of the district can generally find her way through easily opened bridle gates from point to point, from whence, throughout the best part of even a long day, she can witness and enjoy the sport, although she is not with the hounds; and this without pounding on the macadam and shaking her horse's legs; for all our Leicestershire roads are set, as it were, between borders of green velvet in the hunting season. All that is necessary to a most enjoyable day (if it is fine) is a horse that can get over the ground in tiptop form—a good bred one that can gallop and stay. On such a one, lots of grand hunting may be seen if it cannot be done by even a timid lady who dare not essay jumping.

Turning, however, from the delicate and timid to those whose health and physique enable them to hold their own in the front rank, I venture to point out a possible casualty that may happen in hunting, which, although not of frequent occurrence, may easily be attended with dangerous results if the fair rider with hounds is unacquainted with the means of counteracting it. I allude to the possibility of a horse in crossing a ford, where the stream is rapid and the bottom uneven, losing his footing. I have seen this occur more than once, both to good men and to ladies, and the result was not only an immersion over head and ears, but considerable danger as well. This is easily to be prevented, as follows: The fact of a horse losing his footing in deep water is at once apparent by his making a half plunge, and commencing to swim, which instinct teaches him to do directly he feels that he is out of his depth. At such a moment, if the rider confines the horse, he will inevitably roll over in his struggle. The great thing, therefore, on such an occasion is at once to give him his head, quitting the curb rein entirely, and scarcely feeling the snaffle, "while any attempt to guide the horse should be done by the slightest touch possible" (see "Aid Book"). The reins should be passed into the right hand, with which, holding the crop also, the rider should take a firm hold of the upper crutch of the saddle. She should, at the same time, with her left hand raise her skirt well up, disengage her left leg (with the foot, however, still in the stirrup), and place it *over the third crutch*. By these means she will avoid any risk of the horse striking her on the left heel with his near hind hoof, which otherwise in his struggle he would be almost certain to do. If a horse is left to himself he will swim almost any distance with the greatest ease, even with a rider on his back; and there is no more difficulty in sitting on him in the form above named than in cantering on *terra firma*. It is absolutely necessary, however, to get the foot—and especially the stirrup—out of the way, otherwise there is always danger of his entangling himself with them or with the skirt. When the horse recovers his footing on the bottom he will make another struggle, but the hold of the right hand upon the pommel will always preserve the seat of the rider. To be quite safe in such a predicament is simply a question of knowing what to do, and having the presence of mind to do it *quickly*. To show that the necessity for swimming a horse may occur to a lady as well as to a gentleman the following case, I trust, will suffice.

Many years ago I was riding with a lady from the village of Renteria *en route* to San Sebastian, in the north of Spain. The way was round a couple of headlands, between which was a deep bay, running up to the hamlet of Lezo. This bay was all fine sand up to some low but rather precipitous cliffs at the head of the inlet, but at the extremity of either headland careful riding was requisite by reason of rough rocky places. On the occasion I allude to the tide was flowing when we rounded the first point. Having been long accustomed to the place, however, we both considered that we had ample time safely to turn the other extremity of the bay; but a lively spring tide, aided by a brisk north-easterly wind, caused the sea, running in through the narrow gut of "Passages," to increase in velocity to such an extent that we were completely out in our reckoning. Seeing the tide gaining rapidly on us, we set our horses going at top speed over the level sand, racing (as it were) with the "hungry waters" for the distant point. When we neared it, however, I saw at once that it was hopeless to attempt rounding it, for our horses were already above the girths in water, keeping their feet with difficulty on the level sand, and I knew that to try to keep them on their legs on the shelving and rocky bottom at the extremity of the point would result in their rolling over us. There was nothing, therefore, for it but to try back, endeavour to regain the head of the inlet, and make the attempt, however difficult, to clamber up the steep but still sloping face of the cliff. Long before we reached our point, however, both horses were swimming; but they made scarcely a perceptible struggle in doing so, as the rising water lifted them from the level sand bodily off their feet. The lady (who was at first a little flurried) lost no time in getting her habit and her leg out of the way of mischief, and quickly regaining her nerve laid fast hold of the saddle, and laughing, declared it was "capital fun." I confess, on her account, and that of the horses, I did not think so; but encouraged her in her fearlessness. We gave the horses their heads, and they struck out bravely towards the cliff. As soon as they recovered their footing, the lady, having been previously cautioned to extricate her foot from the stirrup, slipped off her horse, the water taking her up to her waist. I lost no time in following her example, and turning the horses loose, we drove them at the sharp and slippery incline up the hill. Both horses scrambled up, with no further damage than the breaking of a bridle; but to get the lady (encumbered as she was with her wet garments) up the steep hillside was a task I have not forgotten to this day. The face of the cliff was studded with patches of gorse here and there, which assisted us certainly at the expense, of my companion, of severely scratched hands and torn gloves. But the ground was so slippery that our wet boots caused us continually to slip back, both of us in this respect being at a great disadvantage with the horses, whose iron shoes and corkings enabled them to obtain better foothold. Partly, however, by dragging, partly by cheering the lady to persevere. I succeeded in gaining the level ground with her, while the sea broke in heavy, noisy surges below, and sent the spray flying over us. The lady, who had borne up bravely so far, fainted from reaction when we gained the level sward, where the horses were grazing quietly, none the worse for their bath. But there were three stalwart Basque peasants at work hard by, turning up the soil with their four-pronged iron forks. Their cottage was close at hand, and having partially revived the fair sufferer, we carried her to the house, where she received every attention from the padrona, and no further evil resulted, except scratches and torn garments. But while I was sensibly impressed with the courage displayed by my companion, who was a slight, delicate woman, I am quite certain that ignorance of the right thing to do at the right time would have been fatal to both of us. As the tide gained so rapidly upon us, had the lady allowed her horse to flounder or plunge in it, she would inevitably have become entangled with him and drowned, despite any effort of mine to save her.

I have witnessed many other instances of the facility with which horses will extricate their riders from difficulties in deep water. Among these I know none more worthy of record than the following.

Some years ago a large Government transport, conveying troops and horses, was wrecked at Buffalo, Cape of Good Hope. Among the troops was a detachment of light cavalry. The ship parted on the rocks, and despite the efforts of the people on shore, the greater part of the troops (officers and men) were drowned. An officer of the cavalry party, however, determined to make an effort to reach the shore, upon which a heavy sea and tremendous surf were breaking. He launched his horse overboard, and, plunging quickly after him into the tumbling sea, seized the horse by the mane, and succeeded in retaining his grasp, while the plucky and sagacious animal gallantly dragged his master in safety through the surf.

I repeat, then, Be always on your guard in crossing deep water with a horse, or in fording a stream where the current is rapid. In India and other tropical countries the necessity for being able to swim a horse occurs more frequently than at home; and, in the monsoon time especially, it behoves everybody who is going a journey on horseback to be extremely careful how they attempt to cross a swollen stream, as the freshets come down with such rapidity that I have frequently seen a horse carried off his legs by the force of the current when the water has not been more than knee-deep, and, when once the foothold is gone in such places, it is extremely difficult frequently to find a place at which to get out again, on account of the precipitous formation of most of the banks. In any case, however, the above-named directions will be found effectual, and the horse, if left to himself, will find a landing place, even if he swims a considerable distance to gain it.

A point of considerable importance as regards hunting also is for ladies to avoid riding home in open carriages, no matter how fine the weather may be, or how well they may be wrapped up. Riding *to* the meet on wheels is all very well, particularly if the distance is great and by a cross-country road, and the time short. But, after galloping about during the greater part of the day, no conveyance home other than her horse is fit for a lady, except the inside of a close carriage on rail or road, and a good foot warmer at the bottom of the carriage; and if there has been much rain, riding home on horseback is by far the safest plan. I have frequently ridden home sixteen and eighteen miles after dark with a lady whom I had the honour of escorting on her hunting excursions, sometimes in very bad weather, and I can safely say that, rain, snow, or sleet, she never took cold. After leaving the hounds my first care was always to make for some hospitable farmhouse near the road, or in default thereof, some decent roadside inn, where we could have the horse's legs well washed, and the lady's waterproof carefully put on if there was rain about. I always carried for her a second pair of dry knee boots, carefully folded up in a waterproof haversack. These boots were made with cork soles within and without, and, as such boots are easily carried by any man who pilots a lady (of course I don't mean the pilot who rides in scarlet), I specially recommend them to consideration. The most difficult thing after riding a long day's hunting, in which, now and again, a good deal of it will be in wet weather, is to keep the feet warm. Throughout all the rest of the system the circulation may be kept going by the exercise even of slow steady trotting; but the wet, clammy boot, thoroughly saturated, it may be, by more than one dash through a swollen rivulet, strikes cold and uncomfortable in the stirrup iron even to a man, who has a better opportunity of counteracting it by the use of alcoholic or vinous stimulants. It is therefore highly conducive to a lady's comfort after her gallop with hounds, if she has far to go home, to change her boots; and this, with a little care and foresight on the part of her attendant, can always be accomplished. With a dry pair of boots, a good waterproof overcoat, and a cambric handkerchief tied round her neck, a lady may defy the worst weather in returning from hunting.

A word now about second horsemen, in a country like this, where the *habitués* of it know tolerably well, if hunting is to be done in a certain district, that a fox, given certain conditions of wind, is most likely to make for certain points, and that if a covert is drawn blank, the next draw will be in a certain locality, it is not difficult for a good second horseman to be ready at hand when the lady requires a fresh charger. But (assuming always that she can afford to have a second horse out) nothing connected with her hunting requires more discrimination than the selection of a second horseman. Any quantity of smart, good-looking, light-weight lads, who can turn themselves out in undeniable form, and ride very fairly, are always to be had, with good manners and equally good characters; but one thing requisite is that they should know every inch of the country they are in. Thus a lad, however willing, from Scotland or Ireland, would be of very little use as a second horseman in the midland district of England; and therefore weight, up to ten stone at all events, is of less consequence than an intimate knowledge of the topography of the surrounding country.

To have a second horse at the right spot at the right time, and with little or nothing taken out of him, requires in most cases considerable foresight and judgment on the part of the lad who is on him, and therefore a fair amount of intelligence, in addition to careful riding, is indispensable, as well as natural good eye for country. The different form in which second horses are brought to the point where they are required is conclusive as to the foregoing, for one constantly sees two animals, up to equal weight and in equal condition, arrive at the same spot, one not fit to go much further, and the other with scarcely the stable bloom off his coat.

CHAPTER XVIII.

The Condition of Hunters.

As the value of most of the foregoing suggestions as regards a lady riding to hounds is more or less dependent upon the form and condition in which the horse destined to carry her in the chase is put, I trust a few words upon this important subject may be acceptable.

In the first place, then, experience proves that the getting of a horse into really good condition is a work of considerable time, and that when once the animal has arrived at the desired point of physical health which will enable him to make the most of his powers, as a rule, it is considered to the last degree undesirable that anything should be done to throw him out of his form.

Many years ago it was considered that a horse that had been hunted regularly through a season should be turned out to grass throughout the summer, and that if he was taken up when the crops were off the ground, there was time enough to get him fit by November; while it was considered altogether unnecessary to give him more than one feed of corn a day while turned out. In numerous cases I have known he had none from April to September.

The present form of treating hunting horses is diametrically the reverse of the foregoing. A horse once "wound up" (as it is technically called) for hunting is generally kept up all the year round; his spring and summer training consisting of long, slow, steady work, principally walking exercise.

Now, my own opinion, based upon many years of experience and close observation, does not agree with either of the foregoing practices.

The first evidently was wrong, because a horse, even running in and out throughout the entire summer, though well kept on corn, will put up an amount of adipose substance, which cannot be got off in two months, with due regard to the preservation of proper quality and muscular fibre. While, on the other hand, I believe that, although by keeping your horse up all the year round you will bring him out in rare form in November, yet still he will not last you so long as one that has had fair play given to his lungs by a few weeks' run when the spring grass is about; for, however good the sanitary arrangements of our modern stables and the ventilation of boxes may be, the air breathed in them cannot be so pure as that of a fresh green meadow. Men and women require a change of air once a year at least, and everybody who can afford it looks forward with pleasurable anticipation to their autumn holiday. Why should the noble animal who has carried us so well and so staunchly through many a hard run be denied his relaxation and his change of air in the spring?

As a substitute for turning horses out for a brief run in the spring, it is customary in some stables to cut grass and give it, varied by vetches and clover, to the horse in his box. These salutary alternatives are good in themselves, but there is still wanting the glorious fresh air of the open paddock, which, when all nature is awakening from the long slumber of winter, is so renovating to the equine system.

It is best to fetch your horse up at night, because it is in the night when turned out that he eats the most; but the object of giving the animal his liberty is not that he may blow himself out with grass, but that, in addition to the purifying effect to the blood of spring herbage, he shall also breathe the spring air unadulterated. If this is carried out, I believe those who practise it will find that their hunters will last them many years longer than those that are kept at what may be called "high stable pressure" all the year round.

Prejudice, however, is strong as regards the foregoing matter, as in others connected with the stable treatment and general handling of horses. People are far too apt to go into extremes and adopt a line of treatment because it is in vogue with some neighbour or friend who is supposed to be well up on the subject, and must therefore be right in everything he does. The best way, I submit, is to call common sense into play, and be satisfied that the oracular friend has some good reason " which will hold water " for what he does.

I respectfully recommend the spring run then, by all means; and, if I may venture so far to infringe the imperious laws of fashion, I would venture to suggest that hunters might be allowed just a little bit more tail, for the purpose for which nature intended it—namely, to keep off the flies, which in summer will find them out, in or out of the stable. Extremes in fashion as to the trimming of horses are nearly as absurd as one sees from time to time in the dress of ladies and gentlemen, and quite as devoid of sense or reason. Who has not seen the old racing pictures in which Diamond or Hambletonian figure with a bob tail, and who has not laughed at the grotesque figure (according to modern notions of a racehorse) of these " high-mettled ones," all but denuded of their caudal appendages?

As a matter of taste and good feeling, therefore, I venture to plead for a trifle more tail for hunters than is at present allowed. To a good stableman it gives no trouble, and in spring and summer time it is of great use to the horse. When the latter is brought up from the spring run, the question of restoring his hunting form (if, indeed, he can be said to have lost any of it) is simple enough; in fact, there are few subjects on which more twaddle is talked than about the "conditioning of hunters," stablemen being particularly oracular and mysterious about it. Roomy, clean, and well-ventilated boxes, good drainage, four and five hours' walking exercise every day, the best oats procurable given *whole, not crushed*, with a moderate allowance to old horses of good beans, and a fair allowance of good old hay or clover, perfect regularity in exercise and stable times, the attendance of a thoroughly good-tempered cheery lad who knows his business, and the total prohibition of drugging or physicking of any sort, unless by order of a veterinary surgeon—these are the arcana of the much talked-of "conditioning." Some tell you that a hunter should have scarcely any hay. I have yet to learn why not, because I am quite sure that really good hay assists a horse to put up muscle. Of course he is not supposed to gorge himself with it, as some ravenous animals would do if allowed. But the same thing may be said of a carriage horse or a charger. Waste of forage is one thing, the use of it another; and as there has been considerable discussion of late as to the cost of feeding a horse, I beg to say that on a fair average those even in training, requiring the best food, can be kept, when oats are 32s. or 33s. a quarter, for 15s. a week. I speak of course of the absolute cost of forage of the best kind.

Where horses are delicate feeders, and this is the case with some who are rare performers in the field, the appetite should be coaxed, by giving small quantities of food at short intervals, making the horse, in fact, an exception to the ordinary stable rule of feeding four times a day. A really good groom will carefully watch the peculiarities of such a horse as regards feeding, and come in due course to know what suits the animal, the result being plenty of good muscle, equal to that of more hearty "doers." But stimulating drugs, I repeat, should never be permitted. Carrots as an alterative are good, but they should be given only when ordered by a veterinary surgeon, in such quantities as he orders. They should be put in the manger whole, never cut up, as there is nothing more dangerous than the latter practice in feeding, because numerous instances are on record of horses choking themselves with pieces of carrot.

When hunting time approaches, a little more steam as regards pace at exercise may be put on. Trotting up hills of easy ascent serves materially to "open the pipes," and, despite a very general prejudice to the contrary, I maintain that, for some weeks before hunting commences, a horse is all the better for a steady canter of moderate length every morning. A very good reason why stud grooms as a rule object to this is, simply because it involves a great deal more work in the stable.

If horses are only walked or trotted at exercise, one man generally can manage very well to exercise two horses, riding one, and leading the other with a dumb jockey or bearing reins on him; but, if the horse is to be cantered, there must be a man or boy to every horse, and, consequently, exercise would occupy considerably more time.

It is quite clear that the horse will have to gallop when hunting begins, and, as all training should be inductive, it is absurd to say that he should do nothing up to the 31st of October but walking and trotting, while on the first day of November his owner may come down from town and give him a rattling gallop with hounds. Surely such extremes are not reconcilable with common sense!

Let me now say a word about washing horses, about which also considerable diversity of opinion exists, some maintaining that the brush and wisp alone ought to keep the horse's skin in proper form, and others advocating washing partially.

In my time I have tried all sorts of stable management, and I believe the truth is as follows: Nothing is more conducive to a horse's health than washing, with either cold or tepid water. But if you adopt the cold water system, you must be sure that it is done in a place where there is no draught. It should be commenced in summer time. There should be two thoroughly good stablemen in the washing box, and a boy to carry water from the pump. The horse's head and neck should be thoroughly washed, brushed, scraped, sponged, and leathered, and a good woollen hood put on. His body washed thoroughly in the same way, and a good rug put on. Then his legs equally well done, and bandaged. Let him then be put into his box for a quarter of an hour or twenty minutes, stripped and dressed by a man who will let his shoulder go at him, not one who will play with him. When thoroughly dressed his coat will shine like new satin, and his whole manner will tell you how refreshed he is by his bath. The washing cannot be done too quickly consistent with thorough good work. Two good men and a smart boy ought to wash, clothe, and bandage a horse in five minutes, or they are not worth their salt.

If the cold water system is begun in summer, and regularly followed up, it can be carried on throughout the winter, no matter how severe the weather may be, and an incalculable advantage of the system is that a horse so treated is almost impervious to cold or catarrh.

But to carry the treatment out, a lot of first-class stablemen are indispensable, men who—no "eye servants"—do their work *con amore*, and take a genuine pride in their horses. If the thing is negligently done, or dawdled over, it is likely enough to be productive of mischief.

Where the stable staff is limited in number and not first-rate in quality, if washing is resorted to, tepid water must be used, because one smart man can wash a horse in tepid water in a proper washing house unassisted. But a special veto should be put upon washing a hunter's legs, as is too often done, outside in the yard, the horse tied to a ring in the wall, with the cold night air blowing on him. No matter if warm or cold water is used, whether or not mischief follows is mere matter of chance if the foregoing bad treatment is permitted.

Briefly, then, it may be said, if you have good men about you and enough of them use cold water, beginning in the summer and continuing it regularly. If you are short of really good stablemen, use tepid water; but use it in a washing box built for the purpose, and never let it be done out of doors.

CHAPTER XIX.

HAVING endeavoured to mark out the course of equitation from the preparatory suppling practices to the orthodox conventionalities of the hunting field, I conclude this series of papers with a few hints which I trust will be useful to ladies about to proceed to India or the colonies.

In the first place, as regards riding habiliments, I recommend ladies going to India to procure everything in the shape of habits, trousers, and hats in this country. In India they cost a hundred per cent. more than at home, and the natives can only make them by pattern. Riding boots can be procured in the East quite as well made and as durable as those made in England, and at a fifth of the price.

Saddlery should be taken out from England. It is also just a hundred per cent. dearer in India. One good side-saddle, such as I have previously described, will with care last a lady many years. Of bridles she should take at least half a dozen double ones (bit and bridoon). Horse clothing of any sort as used in England is not required in India.

As regards the horse itself on which the fair emigrant to the East will take her health-preserving morning gallop at gun-fire, I must say little. I have endeavoured elsewhere to give some idea of what Arab horses are; and, as every lady going to India is certain to know some male friend who is well up at buying a lady's horse, I need only say that, if the animal purchased is a young unbroken one, the best plan is to send him to the nearest cavalry or horse artillery station, and have him broken precisely in the same form as an officer's charger. The Arab dealers from whom the horse, if unbroken, is most likely to be purchased, know nothing, and care less, about breaking, and the people about them have the very worst hands upon a horse I have ever seen.

All riding in India, except in cases of absolute necessity, should be done very early in the morning. The lady should be in the saddle soon after gun-fire (five o'clock). By the time she arrives at the galloping ground (in a large station or cantonment generally the racecourse) the sun will be up, so quickly does it rise, with scarcely any twilight, in India; but its rays are not then vertical, nor is the heat either oppressive or injurious until much later in the day.

A couple or three hours' riding is sufficient for health, and the great thing is to go home quite cool; the bath and breakfast are then most enjoyable. Evening promenades are as a matter of fashion, and indeed, of reason, usually attended by ladies in carriages. There are many, however, who prefer riding on horseback again in the latter part of the day; but experience proves that evening riding on horseback is not good, as a rule, for ladies. Exposure to the sun on horseback, or indeed in any way, should be specially avoided, as should also violent exercise of any kind, that on horseback not excepted. The rattling gallop, which is not only exhilarating but healthful in Leicestershire, is inadmissible in most parts of India, where extremes of any kind are injurious. Finally, I would respectfully impress upon every lady who is likely to go to India, those especially who, having been born there, have been sent home for their education, that they should avail themselves of every opportunity in this country of becoming efficient horsewomen. To be able to ride well is very desirable for a lady who is to pass her life in Europe, in India it is absolutely indispensable; and if the lady's equitation is neglected in early days at home, she will find herself sadly at a loss when she arrives in India; for although there are plenty of thoroughly competent men there who could instruct her, their time is taken up with teaching recruits at the early time of the day at which a lady could avail herself of their services. As regards riding in Australia, the Cape, New Zealand, Canada, or the West Indies, briefly it may be said that again it is best to take out saddlery from this country, because, although it can be procured in any of the above-named colonies far cheaper than in India, it is still considerably dearer, and generally not so good as at home. At the Cape, in Australia, and in New Zealand—the two former colonies especially—long journeys have frequently to be done by ladies on horseback; and if a thoroughly practical education in the saddle is necessary to health, as regards a sojourn in India; it is equally so as a matter of convenience in other of the British dependencies abroad.

Let me, then, close my humble efforts at carefully tracing out the readiest way for a lady to become a thorough horsewoman by again recommending them all to begin early, and to pay implicit attention to the tuition of a first-class instructor; always to throw their whole heart into their riding, fixing their minds rigidly on it while learning, and never, however proficient or confident they may be, venture, unless upon a life-and-death emergency, upon half-broken horses. During the Indian mutiny instances occurred in which ladies owed their lives to their nerve and courage in mounting horses ill-adapted to carry them, and by dint of sheer determination urging them into top speed and safety to the fair fugitives. In such desperate emergencies there is no alternative but to accept the lesser risk; but in ordinary cases my advice (the result of long experience) is to all lady writers, never mount an untrained horse, and never allow your horse to become too fresh for want of work.

A casualty which may be attended with trifling consequences to a man may have the most serious results in the case of a lady; while I am firmly of opinion that no such thing as an accident ought ever to occur to her on horseback if due care and foresight are exercised by those about her, and if the lady herself will be careful whenever or under whatever circumstances she approaches or mounts a horse to be always on her guard, to *ride* all the time she is on him, to remember that in all matters that relate to riding the homely old adage, " Afterwit is not worth a penny an ounce" is strictly applicable, and that the golden rule is, " Never give away a chance to your horse."

www.ingramcontent.com/pod-product-compliance
Lightning Source LLC
Chambersburg PA
CBHW020311170426
43202CB00008B/574